Building the
Northern Rock

'Grey Street, Newcastle upon Tyne' by J. W. Carmichael, one of several locations in the
city centre where the Rock and Northern Counties building societies were to reside.

Building the
Northern
Rock

STEPHEN ARIS

Picture Acknowledgements

We are grateful for permission to reproduce illustrations from the following sources:

Advertising Archives 55 (bottom right), 64 (middle), 67 (top right, both pictures), 76 (middle), 77 (middle), 79 (middle), 81 (top), 82 (bottom 3 pictures), 88 (bottom 3 pictures), 94 (top 3 pictures); Alex Ramsay 23 (inset), 24 (bottom), 31 (top), 32, 36, 41, 44 (bottom), 48, 50 (main), 52 (top), 55 (top), 74, 83 (bottom), 85, 91, 98, 102 (bottom), 105, 108-9, 112, 122-3, 123, 138-9; Arthur Rule (private collection) 104 (bottom), 111; Beamish, The North of England Open Air Museum 34 (bottom) 84 (top); Bridgeman Art Library 9, 11 (bottom), 12, 13 (bottom), 35, 54 (bottom), 61; Camera Press 66 (bottom), 71 (bottom), 94 (bottom), 96, 104 (top), 106; Eleanor Hayes 17, 43 (top), 58 (bottom); Fuller Osborn (private collection) 83 (top), 84 (bottom), 88 (top), 99, 116; Hulton Getty Picture Collection 27, 81 (top), 82 (top); Imperial War Museum 76 (top); Laing Art Gallery/Tyne & Wear Archives 2, 10 (top), 14, 18, 21, 22, 24 (top), 25 (top), 25 (bottom), 30, 31 (bottom), 38, 57 (top 2 pictures), 62 (main), 72; London Transport Museum 68 (top); Lord Ridley (private collection) 78 (both pictures); Manchester Central Library (Local Studies) 11 (top); Mary Evans Picture Library 10 (bottom 2 pictures), 46 (bottom); Monthly Chronicle 44 (top); Mrs Briggs (private collection) 70, 71 (top); Newcastle Central Library (Local Studies Section) 16, 20 (bottom), 26 (bottom), 33 (bottom), 37, 40, 42 (left), 46 (top), 47 (both pictures), 50 (inset), 51 (bottom), 54 (top), 55 (bottom left), 56 (both pictures), 57 (bottom), 59 (bottom), 60 (both pictures), 62 (inset), 64 (bottom), 77 (top), 102 (top); Newcastle Chronicle & Journal 10 (second from top), 51 (top), 52 (bottom), 53 (top), 64 (top), 65, 66 (top), 67 (bottom), 76 (bottom), 77 (bottom), 79 (top & bottom), 80 (both pictures), 89 (top), 103 (all 3 pictures), 114 (bottom); Newcastle University 28-9, 42 (right); Newspaper Library 92 (top -The Times); PA News 128 (top); Robert Harding Picture Library 121 (both pictures); Royal Academy 26 (top), 53 (bottom); Science & Society Picture Library 67 (top left), 69 (bottom), 100-1; Sunderland Art Gallery 33 (top); Walker Art Gallery, National Museums and Galleries of Merseyside 13 (top), 20 (top); West Newcastle Local Studies Society 43 (bottom).

© Northern Rock plc 2000
First Published 2000
ISBN 0907 383 416

Art direction: Hamish MacGibbon
Design: Robin Farrow
Project Editor: Eleanor Hayes
Picture Research Assistant: Sandy Neave

Half-title picture: Entrance to Northern Rock House

Foreword

Writing in the twenty-first century as chairman of an organisation which was founded in the nineteenth century puts me in a very privileged position. One hundred and fifty years of continuous growth and evolution, of dedicated service to the community, of helping ordinary people to enjoy the freedoms which home ownership brings, is the heady backdrop to this journey through history. It is an amalgam of individual stories of the people who created and then took Northern Rock forward to the present day.

One of the buzzwords of the late twentieth and early twenty-first centuries – mutuality – is how it all began in 1850, in Mr Wilcke's Temperance Hotel, when the citizens of Newcastle took up the challenge of Richard Cobden and set about the very creation of home ownership for the common man. That the Northern Counties and (soon afterwards) the Rock building societies were at the forefront of this movement should really come as little surprise to those of us around today who recognise Northern Rock plc as a leading player in today's UK home loans market.

The story of how we came to be here, enjoying our present prosperity, is one of hard work and fun, and rich in colour. I hope you enjoy reading it.

Sir John Riddell
Chairman

Author's and Publishers' Acknowledgements

In researching text and pictures for this book the author and publishers received essential expert advice and unfailing help from many people both in Northern Rock and Newcastle as a whole. In particular they would mention, from Northern Rock: Robert Dickinson, immediate past chairman, Leo Finn, chief executive, Matt Ridley, deputy chairman, Fuller Osborn and Arthur Rule, respectively past chairman and secretary, Libby Ellis-Clark, Helen Illingworth, Michael McCardle, Michael Cullen, David Martin, and Ken Symons. Many professionals made a vital contribution, including Joan Foster of Newcastle University, Dr Bill Lancaster, Director of the Centre for Northern Studies, Northumbria University, Patricia Sheldon, and several colleagues in the Local Studies Unit of Newcastle City Library, and the staff of the Laing Art Gallery, Tyne & Wear Archives, the Discovery Museum, and the Newcastle Chronicle & Journal photo-library.

Contents

1

Hurrah for the Land Society

On a cold winter's day early in January 1846, Richard Cobden and John Bright, the founders of the Anti-Corn Law League, travelled to Newcastle to address a mass meeting. The bells of St Nicholas had been rung at intervals throughout the day and towards evening a band paraded the streets around the Corn Exchange. The two men already had a national reputation and it seemed as if the whole of Newcastle had turned out to hear them. Later that evening Cobden was to say that it was the largest indoor meeting he had ever addressed bar one – and that was in the Free Trade Hall in Manchester.

To keep out the cold, the open entrances of the market had been boarded up; the scene was illuminated by temporary gas lights fitted to the pillars; the speakers' platform was hung with slogans – 'Monopoly injures Trade', 'The Bread Tax is odious, cruel and unjust' – and in front was seating for 2,000 people. By 7 o'clock, the local paper reported that 'every position, either for sitting or standing, appeared to be occupied'.

On the platform was a cross-section of Newcastle's liberal establishment, business and professional men devoted to such radical causes as the abolition of the corn laws, free trade, and electoral reform. But it was Richard Cobden himself that the huge crowd was waiting to see and hear. When Cobden, whose train was late, appeared, 'the meeting', so the *Newcastle Chronicle* reported, 'immediately rose in a body, and greeted him with several rounds of cheers; a cloud of hats and handkerchiefs waving . . . in all directions.'

By January 1846, Cobden's seven-year campaign against the Corn Laws was close to success, as he himself recognised. Acknowledging the warmth and size of his reception, he told the crowd: 'There is certainly a boiling up now, everywhere, that seems to argue that we are coming very near to the

Newcastle, painted by J. M. W. Turner, early nineteenth century.

St Nicholas's Square leading to the Cloth Market. To the left of St Nicholas's Church (later Cathedral) is the Corn Exchange, erected in 1839, where Richard Cobden and John Bright addressed the Free Trade meeting in 1846.

Newcastle Chronicle, 9 January 1846.

FREE TRADE MEETING IN NEWCASTLE.

VISIT OF RICHARD COBDEN AND JOHN BRIGHT, Esqrs.

On Monday evening, a public meeting was held in the Corn Market, in this town, to hear addresses from Messrs. Cobden and Bright, as a deputation from the Anti-Corn Law League, on the present state of the Corn Law question, and on the means of promoting the registration of voters for counties. The occasion was deemed one of triumph, and was preceded by somewhat unusual demonstrations. The bells of St. Nicholas were rung at intervals during the day; and towards evening a band music paraded the streets. Active preparations were commenced in the Corn Market as soon as the usual busy terminated on Saturday. A spacious platform erected at the southern end of the building, in front which were ranged rows of seats capable of accommodating about 2,000 individuals, who, with the exception subscribers to the League fund, were charged (to meet the necessary expenses) for the reserve

John Bright and, *below*, Richard Cobden

end of this matter.' But although Prime Minister Peel was to respond to the pressure by repealing the Corn Laws only months later, the seed that Cobden planted at the Corn Exchange that evening was to grow over the next 150 years into a mighty tree known as Northern Rock.

Cobden devoted most of his long speech to making the case for free trade and the abolition of the hated Corn Laws. In a city that was on the threshold of becoming one of the great powerhouses of Victorian industrial expansion, he presented himself as a friend of the town and an enemy of the country.

I want you to understand your power. The power of the country lies in the towns . . . The intellect, the numbers, the wealth, the industry, all that constitutes the greatness and power of England, lies there . . . The counties belong to you, not you to the counties.

With withering scorn, he described the ruling class as:

men with . . . white cravats, top boots and hunting whips, who meet over their wine and walnuts, and discuss who shall represent the county . . . Don't consult them . . . though they have estates ten miles at a stretch . . . they have no more voice . . . than the man in a fustian jacket that has a vote to record at the poll.

At this point there were loud cries of 'hear, hear'. It was only towards the end that Cobden turned his attention to the subject that interested his listeners most of all: property, house ownership and the vote.

Cobden, who had been MP for Stockport since 1841, was, above all, a campaigner: for free trade, electoral reform, freedom for the colonies, the disestablishment of the Church in England and Ireland and, not least, the repeal of the Corn Laws. But he also had a quite brilliant practical idea that was to have consequences that were to reach far beyond his immediate political agenda. The early history of many leading building societies, including the Abbey National and the Northern Counties, one of the precursors of Northern Rock, was shaped by Richard Cobden.

Despite the great Reform Bill of 1832, property remained the key to the franchise and since the property qualifications in the Act were set high, most working people were still excluded. What Cobden had spotted was that, under a law dating back to Henry VI, any freeholder with 40s. a year in income from property, automatically had a vote. It was, of course, an anomaly. An annual income of 40s. in the fourteenth century was a tidy sum: by the mid-nineteenth century, it was not very much at all: the rental income on a £30 house would suffice. But what was needed was a mechanism to deliver housing to the masses at a price that they could afford. The answer was the freehold land society.

Cobden addressing the Anti Corn-Law League Council in Manchester.

Cobden and Bright's interest in promoting freehold land societies was, of course, political: they were trying to change the political landscape by creating an entirely new class of voter. As an exercise in political gerrymandering, the freehold land movement had, as things turned out, very little effect. But if the freehold land movement was, for the most part, a failure as a piece of political engineering, as a means of promoting house ownership for the less well-to-do, it was a spectacular success, thanks largely to a former apprentice in the fancy trade and reformed alcoholic called James Taylor who, being a practical man, was more interested in the economics than the politics.

Just as Birmingham was the cradle of the building society movement, so it was the birthplace of the freehold land movement. In 1847, Taylor founded the Birmingham Land Society. According to a pamphlet published in 1853 when the land society craze was at its height:

'. . . men with white cravats, top boots and hunting whips . . . Don't consult them . . .' (Portrait of Charles Hogg on his hunter 'Alice Grey', 1839, by John Fernley).

Mr. Taylor had been the purchaser of land more than once, and with the purchase he got an abstract, a legal document, which, when he came to understand it, showed him that he had paid the vendor much more than it cost him. The idea then struck him that as the wholesale price of land was much less than the retail, if the working man could be got to subscribe together a large sum for the purchase of land, they could thus have at wholesale prices a stake in the country and a vote.

'The Gin Shop' by George Cruikshank. The evils of drink was a major theme throughout the nineteenth century. Members of the Newcastle Land Society were mainly supporters of the temperance movement.

The author described the principles behind the scheme:

It is a society for the purchase of land. It involves two commercial principles well understood – that purchasers should buy in the cheapest market, and that societies can do what individuals cannot. Till the movement originated, the purchaser of a small plot of ground had to pay in lawyer's expenses connected with the purchase frequently as much as he paid for the plot itself. A society buys a large piece of ground. They make roads through it; they drain it; they turn it into valuable building land; they thus raise its value; and they divide it amongst their members, not at the price at which each allotment is worth, but at the price at which each allotment has cost. Being also registered under the Friendly Societies Act, the conveyance costs the purchaser generally from 25s. to 30s., thus a plot worth £50 is often put into the fortunate allocatee's hands for half that sum . . . A member generally, if he subscribes for a share of £30, pays a shilling a week and a trifling sum a quarter for expenses. With the money this raised an estate is purchased. It is then cut up into allotments, and balloted for. If the subscriber has paid up, he, of course, takes the land, and there is an end to the matter. If he has not, the society gives him his allotment, but saddled with a mortgage. In some societies the members are served by rotation, and 'first come' are 'first served.' The more generally adopted plan however is division by ballot.

Taylor's idea rapidly caught fire. By the end of the first year, the Birmingham society had established six independent societies in which more than 2,000 members had subscribed for more than 3,000 shares.

Other Midlands towns, such as Wolverhampton, Leicester, and Stourbridge quickly followed. Within two years of the creation of the Birmingham Land Society in 1847, the idea had spread as far south as London (with the formation of the National Freehold Land Society – a parent of the Abbey National) and as far north as Newcastle (with the creation of the Newcastle upon Tyne and Northern Counties Freehold Land Society – a precursor of Northern Rock). By 1852, there were 130 land societies with 85,000 members throughout England and the press was beginning to take notice. Not all were friendly. The *Spectator* called it 'a middle-class movement' and *The Times* took it upon itself to warn that 'working classes were being deluded by it'. As *The Times* had few working-class readers, this remark might seem somewhat patronising. What is certainly true, is that the societies were middle class in origin and membership and that for all the populist propaganda the houses built by the land societies were largely beyond the reach of the average Victorian working family.

The Newcastle upon Tyne and Northern Counties Freehold Land Society, to give it its full title, was formed in March 1849 with the object of

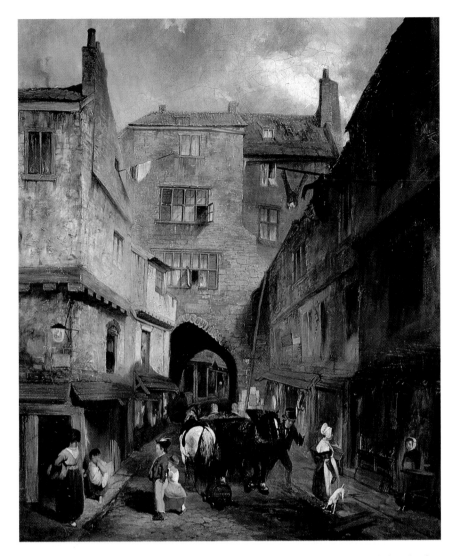

'The Black Gate', Newcastle, looks romantic enough in this painting by George Balmer, but it was to remain a slum area through most of the nineteenth century.

Despite the worthy egalitarian ideals of the Friendly Society movement, it was essentially prosperous middle class in character. The majority of the population, such as these miners at Blaydon Main, painted by Ralph Hedley, could not aspire to house purchase for a century or more.

purchasing land on which to build houses for the deserving and the thrifty. The pace was set by the local Whig politicians. The leading figures were Sir John Fife, an eye surgeon by profession, who had led the great demonstration on the Town Moor in favour of the 1832 Reform Bill, and the local MP, Thomas Headlam, a barrister, who had wrested his Newcastle seat from the Tories in 1847, thus giving the Whigs control of the city. Despite five attempts by the Tories and the Radicals to unseat them, the Whigs ruled Newcastle for the next 18 years, though Headlam did not lose his own seat until 1874.

The committee of the Land Society was a mixture of professional and tradespeople. There were, inevitably, several solicitors and accountants, but there was also a printer, a newsagent, a dyer, and a flour dealer. In their first report, published in July 1850, they wrote:

The committee have great confidence in the Freehold Land Movement, and are strongly impressed with a sense of the social advantages and

'Entrance to Sunderland Harbour' by J. W. Carmichael, 1862.
Shipping, shipbuilding, engineering and mining generated the
spectacular growth of Newcastle and her sister towns of the
north east in the second half of the century.

benefits it confers, and the excellent investment it presents to the working class for their surplus earnings. The peculiar advantage of this investment arises from the great difference between the wholesale and retail prices of land. The committee trust that members will persevere in their laudable purpose until they all shall obtain allotments, and thus secure a sure and unmistakable interest in the property of the country, and that members will not be content with promoting their own welfare, but use their best endeavours to induce their friends to co-operate with us in promoting such a desirable object.

The land chosen for this exciting and uplifting venture was a plot in Gateshead called the Tenement. Formerly part of the Ellison estates, and situated at the junction of the Old Durham Road and the high road to Felling, the estate was renamed Mount Pleasant. There, on a slope above the town, overlooking the river, a local builder, Charles Crawford, was commissioned to lay out the roads and build the detached stone villas for the society's 160 members. Later came two small Methodist chapels and a post office.

The society got off to a promising start. The first – and as it turned out, the last – annual report of the society published in July 1850 reported that an impressive £1,729 16s. 9d. had been raised in subscriptions, and that, after expenses of £209 7s. 1d. there was £1,651 8s. 8d. in the bank, the equivalent of £81,258 in today's money. The committee regretted that some 200 of the original 760 shares had lapsed because the subscriptions had not been paid, and others had not been taken up 'on account of want of employment, emigration and other causes'. The total number of members on the roll was 337 who held a total of 426 shares which were, the committee said, now changing hands at premiums of between 10s. and £2 10s. each. Subscribers paid an entrance fee of 1s., and 3s. each fortnight thereafter.

Five months later the project was complete. On 28 December 1850, the society, having assembled at the Lecture Room in Nelson Street at 2 p.m., set off in a procession led by Mr Headlam and Sir John Fife across the new High-Level Bridge to inspect their new possession. On entering the field, the members were greeted with a salute of cannon after which the dignitaries climbed on to a wagon that was being used as a platform and made, so the local paper reported, 'some appropriate remarks upon the beautiful situation'. In the evening, everybody gathered again at the Lecture Room for a public meeting. Richard Cobden apologised for his absence but sent a message in which he said: 'I am more and more in love with these Freehold Land Societies which both politically and morally are, I think, destined to grow in importance and usefulness.'

Mr J. Williams of Sunderland told the meeting that he had calculated that if the £240,000 which he reckoned was spent in strong drink in Newcastle in a year was spent instead on purchasing freehold allotments at £25, 10,400 freehold votes would be created: 'Join the Freehold Land Society and invest

Built up area:
Before 1830
Before 1858
Before 1894
Before 1921

Newcastle's growth between 1830 and 1921. The shaded sections including Jesmond, Elswick and others indicate the rapid increase in housing fuelled by burgeoning industry in the second half of the nineteenth century.

in it the money hitherto invested in the pipe and the bottle,' he urged. It was an evening for lofty sentiments – none higher than those of William Lockey Harle, the society's solicitor, an ardent Liberal and later a considerable figure in Newcastle politics. His speeches on the Coal Duty, the Team Valley Railway, the Tyne Conservancy Bill and the purchase of the Newcastle Gas Works by the Corporation were considered to be the best speeches delivered by one man in Newcastle Council. He was, it seems, a brilliant conversationalist and a thoroughly engaging man. 'Nothing can exceed the lively rattle of Mr Harle's private conversation,' wrote a local author. 'His animal spirits are boundless and his love of fun literally inexhaustible.'

Having paid tribute to James Taylor, 'the ingenious artisan of Birmingham', William Harle said of Mount Pleasant that he believed that 'the place would be marked in the history of these northern climes and men hereafter would say that they were brave men who laid the foundations of these stones of liberty'. He expressed the hope that the allotments 'would not be made a mere matter of bargain and sale; but that they would be treasured by their possessors as a means of supporting the rights and liberties of their country'. He ended with the hope that when the original 160 died 'others will take their places and carry on that progress which will end only with the mighty destinies of this great land'. He sat down to 'loud and continuous applause'.

The new society was praised in song as well as speech. Sung to the tune of 'The King of the Cannibal Islands' it went (roughly) like this:

Oh! hev ye hear the news se grand,
Aboot a greet big lump 'o land,
I' the Land Society.

And then the Charter we will gain,
That's been se lang wor grief an' pain,
Oh! then we'll sing wivoot disdain,
Success to the Land Society.

I' the public houses aw declare,
Ye'll niver get the Charter there,
Then leave them stannin' where they are,
An' join wor new Society.

Noo werkin', if ye be wise,
Agyen strang drink shut mooth and eyes,
An' then aw'm sure ye'll gain a prize,
All in the Land Society.

So noo, before aw close maw sang,
Aw hope aw'll see ye in' the thrang,
Yor hyems all i' the list so lang,
All in wor new Society.

'Howkey Powkey' Wilcke said,
How will ye hev yor money paid:
Eighteenpence a week they pray'd,
Then hurrah! for the Land Society.

The Lecture Room, Nelson Street, where members of the Land Society assembled before proudly setting off to view their first development in Gateshead.

'Grainger Street, Newcastle upon Tyne', a watercolour painted by T. M. Richardson in 1838.
Northern Counties' first office was located here, in the premises of accountant Charles Burney.

For all the euphoria, the life of the Newcastle Land Society was destined to be short. By the end of the new year, it had disappeared only to immediately reappear as the Northern Counties Permanent Benefit Building Society. It was not the first building society in the north-east – that distinction goes jointly to the Gateshead Building Society and its neighbour the Friendly Building Society that date from 1825. But it was certainly the first permanent building society on Tyneside.

Building societies were, of course, far from unknown in Victorian England. By 1850 historians calculate that there were at least 1,500. The first, Ketley's Building Society, appeared in Birmingham in about 1775. The first building societies were essentially savings clubs in which a small group of local people subscribed a modest sum each week. When enough money had been collected to finance the project, the houses were distributed either by ballot or on a first-come first-served basis and the society was wound up. They were known as terminating societies and had an average life of about ten years. In 1850, nearly all of the 1,500 or so building societies were of this type. But from the late 1840s onwards the idea began to take hold that building societies should no longer lead this ad hoc, butterfly existence but should have instead a continuing life. They were therefore known as permanent building societies.

Historically, the important difference between the two types of building society was that while borrowers and investors in the older form of society were very often, but not always, the same people, in the post-1850 form, the two classes were separate: the personal link was broken and so, in effect, the modern building society was born. From the very earliest days the accent was on raising money, rather than lending it. And it was this that gave the permanent building society a much harder, more commercial edge than the mutual land societies. One can argue, as people did, that building societies were, in the true sense, not mutual at all.

Under the 1836 Building Society Act the societies were forbidden to own land. It was James Taylor, the 'ingenious artisan of Birmingham', who thought of a neat way round this little difficulty. His solution was to combine the work of the freehold land society with that of the building society. Under Taylor's scheme, the freehold land society bought and developed the land while the building society lent the money to buy the houses. In that way, everybody, including the regulators, was happy. The fact that, in many cases, the membership of the land society and the building society often overlapped didn't seem to matter. Of the 34 people who ran the Land Society, just under a quarter of them moved across to become directors of the new building society.

John Mawson, one of the founders and a trustee of the Land Society was a natural choice to be its first chairman. Born in Penrith and a chemist by trade, his early ventures in business both in Sunderland, where he started out, and in Newcastle, were unsuccessful. Matters were made worse when he agreed to underwrite a friend's debt who then refused to honour it. He

'Poor Relations' by Kilburne, perhaps typifies the self-confident and high-minded middle classes who were able to buy their own houses.

worried greatly about money. 'I shall be eighty before I pay off all I owe,' he complained. But after he started to sell Rothwell's Fire Fuel, on which he took out a patent, and became the first importer of German yeast in the north-east, his fortunes revived to such a degree he managed to pay off all his debts before his fortieth birthday. His creditors were so grateful that they presented him with a shelf full of valuable books. He later went into business with his brother-in-law, Joseph Wilson Swan, who became world-famous as the inventor of the incandescent electric lamp. Thanks to Swan, Newcastle was the first city in Britain to be illuminated by electric light.

Radical politics, Low Church beliefs and a visceral horror of the evils of strong drink were the defining characteristics of the building society pioneers of the city of Newcastle. A zealous teetotaller, Mawson travelled the north-east preaching the temperance message to the pitmen. But he was also a very active local politician. Elected to the council for the West All Saint's ward, one of the city's radical strongholds, he eventually rose, just before his death in a tragic accident, to become Sheriff of Newcastle. But his interests were far wider than local politics and local affairs. A personal friend of William Lloyd Garrison, the American advocate of Negro rights, he was a passionate opponent of slavery and an ardent

'Quayside, Newcastle upon Tyne'
Arthur E. Grimshaw, 1895.

Facing page: Joseph Swan (*inset*) was the inventor of the incandescent electric lamp and thus his home city, Newcastle, was the first to be illuminated by electricity. He was a business partner of John Mawson, a Land Society founder, and first chairman of Northern Counties. Their business premises are on the left of this photo of Hood Street, taken in 1912.

supporter of the Union cause in the American Civil War. When the war ended in 1865, Mawson invited Garrison to Newcastle where a soirée was held in the Assembly Rooms in his honour.

The majority of Mawson's co-directors were established local tradesmen, thrifty, hard-working, and conscientious people with a lively sense of public duty. One such was William Brogg Leighton, a bookseller and printer in Grainger Street who also sold country butter and eggs on market days. Leighton was one of the old school of master printers who believed that the only suitable colour for a necktie was white – a colour he wore to the day of his death in 1884.

He was one of the founders of the Newcastle Temperance Society. He signed the pledge in 1835 when he was 25 and married the first Newcastle woman to sign. He was a member of the Newcastle Board of Guardians, and worked as an officer and a promoter of building societies all his life. He was a prominent figure in Primitive Methodism and Sunday School work in the east end of Newcastle. It was therefore entirely appropriate that the first meeting of the new society should be held in a temperance hotel.

Royal Arcade where Northern Counties held its first meeting in Mr Wilcke's
Temperance Hotel. The photo inset on the right shows the modern
reproduction of the interior. (Watercolour by J. Dobson, 1831.)

2

At Mr Wilcke's Hotel

The first meeting of the Northern Counties Permanent Benefit Building and Investment Society took place on Monday 16 December 1850 and was held at Mr Wilcke's Temperance Hotel in the Royal Arcade, Pilgrim Street, in the centre of Newcastle. The hotel survived until 1962 when it was demolished to make way for Swan House.

The first task was to draw up the rules. But apparently the twelve directors did not find it so easy: it was, so the minutes record, the subject of 'protracted discussion'. There is no mention of what caused the difficulty: it may simply have been that there was an awful lot of ground to cover.

The thirty-three rules, which run to thirty-five pages, are comprehensive, covering every eventuality from the time and place of the meetings to the removal of directors. Anybody who refused to serve as chairman, vice-chairman or as a director after having been elected or who resigned 'without sufficient cause to satisfy the directors', would be fined five shillings, and women and minors were barred as officers of the society. As it turned out, women had a long wait. It was not until 1999, a century and a half after the Northern Counties had become Northern Rock and Northern Rock had become a publicly quoted company, that the first woman, Nichola Pease, was appointed to the board as a non-executive director.

From the start it is clear that the new society was a rather different animal from its parent, the Land Society. The tradespeople and shopkeepers were in a majority on the board and it was they who set the tone this time, rather than the politically motivated lawyers and other professionals. Much less was to be heard about providing decent housing for the deserving poor, and much more about the excellent returns available on a pre-eminently safe investment. The accent was more on money and its accumulation than on land and its development, although it is interesting to note that the 'investment' part of the title was dropped almost immediately.

RULES.

Name and Object.

I.—1. This Society shall be denominated "THE NORTH-ERN COUNTIES PERMANENT BENEFIT BUILDING ~~BENEFIT~~ Society".

2 That its object is for raising, by the weekly contributions of the members, a stock or fund, to enable each of them to erect or purchase a dwelling-house or dwelling-houses, or other real or leasehold property.

Time and Place of Meetings.

II —1. The society shall commence on Saturday, the 4th day of January, 1851, and that each member's term of subscription shall be during the one hundred and sixty six lunar months next following the time of payment of his first subscription, or until the invested share shall have realized, by the accumulation of principal, interest, and profits, the sum of £120, when the amount thereof shall be paid to the investing member; and the weekly subscriptions shall be payable at such times and places, as the Directors for the time being shall appoint. The Annual Meeting shall be held in the month of January in each year, at such place as the Directors shall appoint, of which seven days' notice shall be given by the Secretary to each member.

Officers of the Society.

III.—The affairs of the society shall be conducted according to the Rules, by 3 Trustees, 2 Stewards, 12 Directors, a Treasurer, one or more Surveyor or Surveyors, a Solicitor, 3 Auditors, and a Secretary. These Officers, with the ex-

Above: first page of the Northern Counties *Rule Book* and, *right:* an extract from the minutes of its inaugural meeting.

Grainger Market, one of the many magnificent buildings in Richard Grainger's development of central Newcastle.

At a Meeting of the Members of the Northern Counties Permanent Benefit Building Society held at the Temperance Hotel, Royal Arcade, Newcastle on Monday the 16th December 1850. Mr William Veatch in the Chair

The Members proceeded with the consideration of

Nonetheless the rules made it quite clear that housing was the business of the day. They stated that the object of the society was 'for raising, by the weekly contributions of the members, a stock or fund, to enable each of them to erect or purchase a dwelling house or dwelling houses, or other real or leasehold property'. It was agreed that the society would be open for collection of subscriptions on Saturday, 4 January 1851. And although the society, in common with others, quite rapidly developed more efficient methods of collecting money from investors, the weekly subscription remained a key element of the business for many years.

What the society was offering the savers and homeowners of Newcastle was a mortgage and savings product (to use a thoroughly modern term) rolled into one. The society issued shares at a nominal value of £120 apiece for which members would pay a weekly subscription of 2s. 6d. (12.5p). The names of those wanting an advance for a house would be put into a ballot. Applications were dealt with in the order they came out of the hat: the lucky ones got their money early, while the less fortunate had to wait. This system was skewed in favour of the original members and there was therefore some concern that potential investors who joined later might be put off by having to wait until the first-comers had been served. The only way to keep everybody happy, the directors quickly realised, was to beat the drum and keep the money rolling in. By early March, less than two months after opening for business, a subcommittee was inquiring about the cost of advertising in such local papers as the *Newcastle Courant*, the *Newcastle Guardian*, the *Newcastle Chronicle*, the *Gateshead Observer*, and the *Shields Gazette*.

For many years, the directors personally approved every single mortgage application, the details of which were meticulously recorded in the minutes. The secretary had two ledgers, a waste minute book for taking notes of board meetings, and a formal record in which the proceedings of the day were inscribed on lined paper in the secretary's best copperplate. Bound in leather with hand-tooled gold engraving, the official minute books were so large and heavy that the average office junior would have had a hard time lifting them.

Once an application for a mortgage advance had been approved, the money would be released. Meanwhile the mortgagor would continue to pay the weekly 2s. 6d. subscription until the loan was paid off. Alternatively, the subscriber could simply pay the subscriptions without ever applying for an advance. After 160 months, or when the value of the share 'by accumulation of principal, interest and profits,' had reached its nominal value of £120, whichever came first, the money would be repaid, plus interest, as a paid-up share. This meant that over a period of 13.3 years investors would see a minimum of 43.7 per cent return on their money – more if the building society did well. While the rewards were hardly spectacular, as the banks were scarcely in the retail lending business 150 years ago and the stock market was a closed shop for the well-to-do, the new building societies offered the small saver as much security and better returns than such institutions as the trustee savings banks, the benefit societies and the savings clubs.

The society began by offering its investors a return of 4 per cent, plus expenses and a share of the profits. Although the rules mention the P-word from the outset, in the accounts the commonly used term was 'surplus' and, later, 'reserve fund'. Unlike many of the new permanents, the Northern Counties was a genuine mutual in that it treated its lenders and borrowers equally.

In some important respects, the Northern Counties was more flexible and more imaginative than its twentieth-century counterparts. To those building their own house, the society offered 'staging finance', where the money was released in stages as the building went up, floor by floor. Also, the mortgages were transferable, both from mortgagor to mortgagor and from house to house.

In 1851, Newcastle was still a comparatively small place. At 87,000, the population was barely a quarter of what it is today and most people lived in a small but densely packed area in the lower town along the steep banks of the Tyne. The first large-scale Ordnance Survey map, published in 1858, shows that the streets and houses extended from Arthur's Hill in the west to the Byker ropery in the east, and from Brandling Place in the north to the Tyne in the south. But the thrust northwards to Jesmond and east and west towards Byker and Elswick had hardly begun. That was not to say that the town was dormant – far from it. Richard Grainger, the builder and developer, had changed the appearance of the upper town. Many of Newcastle's grandest streets and finest façades date from this period – as does the High-Level Bridge, the Central Station, the Theatre Royal, and the Grainger Market.

None of this would have happened had not the local authority the confidence and the imagination to finance the work which was far beyond Grainger's means. The scale and spaciousness of this redevelopment, the use of

Richard Grainger, whose great project transformed the appearance of Upper Town – fine visitas and buildings that are the glory of the city to this day.

Contemporary painting by Parker of the opening banquet for Grainger Market.

'The Outcast' by Richard Redgrave. The majority of the urban population had to endure slum housing of the kind typified by Castle Garth, c. 1888 (*opposite*) in Newcastle, and (*below*) Gateshead's notorious Pipewellgate, where in 1843 there were just three privies for 2,000 inhabitants.

ashlar sandstone blocks and classical styles signalled unmistakably the arrival of a new middle class determined to make its mark. The rebuilding of Newcastle heralded the coming of a new age. Hitherto the county had been in charge: now it was the turn of the town.

But not everything was bright and beautiful. The heart of the town remained, so the local historian, Sidney Middlebrook, says: 'a thick cluster of chares, courts, passages and narrow streets'. As yet the town had not spread very far beyond the medieval city walls.

In the mid-nineteenth century, Tyneside had the unenviable reputation of having some of the worst slums anywhere in Britain. The overcrowding in the rookeries on the banks of the Tyne was appalling. Robert Rawlinson, an inspecting engineer, wrote of Gateshead in 1850:

> Neither plan nor written description can adequately convey to the mind the true state and condition of the room tenements and of the inhabitants occupying them. The subsoil on the sloping side of the hill is damp and most foul, the brickwork of the buildings is ruinous, the timber rotten; and an appearance of great decay pervades the whole district. The buildings fronting to Hillgate have originally been erected as residences of a superior character, the stairs have carved balusters; the rooms have been fitted up with various forms of decoration, which only serve at present to heighten the grim misery which pervades them. Single rooms are let off as tenements which are crowded with men, women and children; the walls are discoloured with age, damp, and rot; the windows are broken, old rags, straw and boards occupying the place of glass, so that means of light and ventilation alike are absent.

But side by side with the poverty and the squalor was great energy and

expansion. Something of this vigour and optimism is captured in an advertisement that John Benson & Co., tea dealers and fruit merchants of 6 Grainger Street, took to celebrate the opening of the High-Level Bridge.

This auspicious event, so long anticipated, will introduce a New Era into the commercial habits of the adjoining county; and the inhabitants of Gateshead and North Durham will henceforth more fully realise the Advantages of the great trading Establishments of this flourishing Town. It is simply requisite to announce to the intelligent Inhabitants south of the Tyne that the system upon which our Establishment has secured popular Favour in the North is pre-eminently that of keeping a well-selected GENUINE STOCK; whilst others quote prices, WE QUOTE QUALITY and no temporary purpose shall ever induce us to pander to the adulterating and gammoning of the pretending Cheap Houses who sell at such AWFUL SACRIFICES.

This confidence was well-placed. In 1850, Tyneside was on the threshold of an industrial boom that would transform the city and make Tyneside one of fastest-growing areas in the country. The mining industry, the heavy engineering works and the shipyards changed the face of Newcastle and altered the lives of its inhabitants for ever. Slowly at first, and then at an increasing pace, the working people moved eastwards and westwards along the Tyne to take up jobs in the new factories and yards being built on the river bank. With the factories came row upon row of terraced housing. The terraces climbed the steep slopes above the Scotswood Road, looking down on Sir William Armstrong's Elswick works, while further to the west in Benwell, new homes were built to house the skilled engineering workers fleeing the overcrowded tenements of the city centre. With, as yet, no public transport, people needed to live as close to their work as possible.

The market for private houses was still very small. The vast majority of the new housing was built for rent and much of it was put up by the employers themselves to attract the labour they needed. But there was still

J. W. Carmichael's panorama of Newcastle, from Gateshead, in 1846, predating the completion of the High-Level Bridge in 1849.

plenty of scope for private initiative – and for the new building societies which were tailor-made to cater for the needs of the growing middle class and the aspirant skilled working man and his family.

The Northern Counties began cautiously. It was not until December 1854 – four years after its inception – that it rented its first premises in Grainger Street at the offices of its first secretary, Charles Burney Jnr., who had occupied the same position on the board of the Land Society. An accountant by profession, Burney had a handsome house in Gateshead and was for many years the treasurer of the Gateshead Council. This was the beginning of a Burney family connection with Northern Counties that was to last for more than 80 years!

Unquestionably the key man in the business was the secretary, even though in the early years he, like everyone else, was a part-timer. The title is misleading. In effect he was the chief executive. He was not only the keeper of the society's records but also its guardian, ever-mindful of the best interests of the society. The watchword was safety first. The rules laid down that:

> the Secretary shall give immediate information to the chairman of anything that may come to his knowledge which he apprehends will be of advantage or disadvantage to the Society, in order that the chairman may deliberate on the necessity of taking immediate

John Dobson's Central Station, 1863 (*facing page*), and today.

measures and calling a special board of Directors, and that they may withhold payment of any award, should any doubts present themselves as to the security being sufficient.

The secretary was not paid a salary but as an incentive to drum up business received a commission of 1*s.* 6*d.* for every share subscribed.

The big event in the society's calendar was the weekly subscription meeting at which the society's stewards were on hand to collect the cash as it came through the door. The first sums were not large: in the first month of its life, January 1851, the society collected all of £92 0*s.* 6*d.* By the end of February, the directors were pleased to report that there was already over £250 in the bank. By the end of the year, subscription income had risen to the grand total of £1,603 19*s.* 6*d.*, while £1,590 11*s.* 9*d.* had been lent out in mortgage advances. The bill for salaries was £21 8*s.* 10*d.* and postage and sundries came to £3 6*s.* 5*d.* Overall there was a balance of £25 12*s.* 6*d.* The society was just about in profit.

An indication of just how quickly the society was moving away from its radical origins came very early on. The society was hardly a month old, when a row broke out about the allocation of advances. At the board meeting on 25 January 1851, a ballot had been taken to determine the order in which applicants for advances should be dealt with. There were six names in all. The first out of the hat was Joseph Davison, one of the

John Dobson, one of the leading architects of Grainger's project. His buildings include the Royal Arcade, as well as the station and other structures.

founders of the Land Society who had a grocer's business in Churchill Street and was later a chairman of the society: he wanted the tidy sum of £600. So did Alexander Guthrie, another Land Society pioneer. But it was the application by William Young Robson, who had a flour business in the Groat Market, for ten shares worth £1,200 that was most remarkable. (In modern money, the equivalent of some £54,000). It was enough to buy him at least half a dozen terraced houses.

Precisely what caused the stir is not recorded. But feelings ran high. Thomas Galloway, who had come fifth in the ballot, felt so aggrieved that he wrote to the directors saying that unless the first ballot was annulled, he would appeal to arbitration. And one of the directors, Andrew Middlemas, the auditor, put forward a motion declaring the ballot to be illegal. Faced with pressure from the members and a split in their own numbers, the directors agreed that there should be a new ballot on 27 February and that all applications received in the post up to that date should be included.

The second ballot was more even-handed. This time thirty people were awarded advances which ranged from five shares at £120 each to one-fifth of a share worth £24. William Robson got £600 – half what he asked for last time – while Joseph Davison's position was unchanged. Not surprisingly, some of the money raised was spent on houses at the Land Society's Mount Pleasant estate but the society was equally happy to finance the directors' own less modest projects. In May, the directors agreed to lend their fellow director, William Veatch, £540 on a house and garden in Bensham worth, the members of the survey committee estimated, £600, while Alex Guthrie received a £350 loan on a house in the Scotswood Road.

John Mawson had been in office for only a year when on 21 January 1852 he was succeeded as chairman by Matthew Reed. A builder by trade with a business in Bath Road, Reed was to be the dominant figure in the society's affairs for the next eleven years. Of the eighty-four board meetings between 1851 and 1858 he missed only seven. To judge from the quantity and the size of the advances that Reed obtained it is plain that he saw the society more as an adjunct of his business than as a philanthropic venture. Between 1852 and 1863 he asked for loans worth over £100,000 in modern money on houses along the Scotswood Road. But he was not alone. Other directors, as well as Charles Burney, the secretary, and William Lockey Harle, the solicitor, built up substantial property portfolios with money borrowed from the society.

If the society was to prosper and to meet the pressing demands for loans, it was clear it could not simply rely on subscriptions alone. The rules had been drafted to allow the society's trustees to borrow, provided that the total sum did not exceed two-thirds of the amount out on mortgage. At a

'Murton Colliery' by J. W. Carmichael. Mining was central to the north-east's industrial development.

Facing page: Grey's Monument commemorating the enactment of the Reform Bill and Lord Grey as the champion of civil and religious liberty.

William Lockey Harle, the Northern Counties Society's first solicitor, whose dubious mixing of personal interest with business would lead him into trouble.

The second half of the nineteenth century saw huge industrial growth in the north east, expressed by William Bell Scott's painting 'Industry of the Tyne: Iron and Coal', 1861 (*facing page*).

Above: Mitchell's Low Shipyard in the 1850s

Below: the collier *John Bowes* launched at the Jarrow yard of Palmer Bros and Co.

meeting on 27 March, 1851, the board decided that the finance committee should try and identify possible lenders and that the trustees should be empowered to borrow money not exceeding twice the amount in hand at the time and at a rate not more than 5 per cent. An offer from William Harle, the society's solicitor, of £500 at 5 per cent was already on the table. Harle's heart may well have been in the right place but as he was asking 1 per cent over the rate the society was paying ordinary investors he did to not allow sentiment to overrule his business sense.

In December 1857, Harle wrote to the board asking if he could borrow money against the society's bills and suggested that in the first year he should be charged at the rate of 1 per cent instead of the customary 2 per cent. The directors agreed in principle but refused his request for preferential treatment and asked that he guarantee that he would renew those bills that were not taken up by the society when they fell due.

Harle's propensity for mixing personal and official business was later to lead him into trouble. The board minutes for 11 January 1864 record that the directors met in Temperance Hall, Nelson Street, in pursuance of a requisition signed by the directors for 'the purpose of removing Mr William Lockey Harle from his office as solicitor to this Society and electing another solicitor.' The previous month, the board had said that, having investigated the case against the solicitor, it was of the opinion that a case of 'great carelessness and irregularity' had been made out. The minutes do not say exactly what Harle had done but they do give a clue. Harle had, so the directors believed, broken rule 6 which states: 'That if the Treasurer or Trustee or any other Director or (sic) officer of this Society, shall neglect to pay over monies received by them . . . he or they be fined for and in respect of the same default 25 per cent on the amount detained.' It was only after Jacob Weir, the treasurer, had argued in favour of a fine rather than dismissal that Harle kept his job.

This was the second boardroom upset within a year. Twelve months previously, in January 1863, Matthew Reed suddenly resigned after 11 years in the chair. There is no mention in the minutes as to why Reed felt he had to go but it was clearly unexpected. At their January meeting, the directors failed to pass the customary motion thanking the outgoing chairman for his services: even stranger, there was no vote of thanks at that month's annual general meeting. It rather looks as if Matthew Reed left under something of a cloud. His

immediate successor, Ralph Cook, a butcher, served only a year, and on 30 January 1864, the society turned, once again, to its first chairman, John Mawson. Unhappily, his tenure too was to be all too brief.

Despite these troubles, the society itself was prospering. Ten years before, in March 1853, it had made the very first of what was to be a long list of takeovers by absorbing the Albion Permanent Building Society at its own request. For this privilege, the Albion had to pay a premium of £20! By 1855, the word was being spread at public meetings in outlying villages; the House of Commons was petitioned against the imposition of stamp duty on building societies; and the range of its activities had spread as far as Scotland. In August 1861, the secretary reported that he had received an application for an advance of £2,800 on a property in Glasgow. In the same month, the board was exploring the idea of renting the ground floor of Charles Burney's Grainger Street office at a cost of £70 a year.

After 10 years in business, the Northern Counties was lending as far north as Newbiggin-by-the-Sea in Northumberland on a fish-curing establishment and as far south as Harrogate where it advanced £1,920 on four houses and shops. The annual report for 1862 shows that since it began the society had advanced a total of £124,500 and that the profit on each original share amounted, with interest and expenses, to £8 19s. 6d. In introducing what was to be his last report, Matthew Reed said: 'The Directors have considerable pleasure in directing the attention of Members to the large increase in, and the profitable nature of the operations and general business of the Society . . . These operations realise a result which the Directors doubt not will be considered by the Members as it is by them very gratifying and satisfactory.'

The Northern Counties was leading the way but its example had been quickly followed. Between 1851 and 1872 some fourteen other building societies appeared in Newcastle. Among them, the Crown Benefit (1851), the Star (1860), Newcastle and Gateshead Permanent Benefit (1864), and, most important for our story, the Rock Permanent Benefit (1865). As the 1870s approached, a house-building boom was gathering pace and the mood among Newcastle's infant building societies was one of great optimism.

After ten years in business, the Northern Counties was lending as far north as Newbiggin-by-the-Sea in Northumberland, photographed (*above*) towards the end of the nineteenth century.

Facing page: The Theatre Royal, Grey Street, built for Richard Grainger by John and Benjamin Green 1836–7.

3
Steady, Continuous and Satisfactory Progress

Like the Northern Counties 15 years previously, the Rock Building Society held its first meeting in a temperance hotel in January 1865. The place chosen was Mr Bell's in West Clayton Street – which still exists very much in its original form. The founders of the Rock were fairly similar in outlook and background to the Northern Counties' men. The three trustees were George Weatherhead, paper-stainer, of West Clayton Street, George Hedley, cattle salesman, of Westmoreland Terrace, and James Henry Tate, builder, of Elswick.

Amongst the directors were three builders, two accountants, an auctioneer, a tea dealer, a timber merchant, a brush manufacturer, a draper, a watch-maker, and an architect. The solicitor was Robert Dickinson, whose family was, over the next four generations, to have an enormous influence on the history and development of the Rock.

A retiring, bookish man who, according to his son, liked nothing more than 'to get away in some quiet corner and read', Robert seems to have been a late developer, largely by reason of chronic ill-health. When he was 23, he was obliged to leave the harsh climate of the north-east for a tour of France and Italy (the original plan was to go to India but the ship was too heavily laden and had to turn back).

But the years 1865 and 1866 marked the beginning of a new and more vigorous phase. In 1865, as well as becoming the Rock's solicitor, he took up the post of deputy coroner, a job that took him all over the county. In May of the following year, he married Jane, one of the Harle clan, daughter of George Harle, an iron merchant. Like most other professional people on Tyneside at that time, Robert was, according to his son, a 'strong Liberal who took an active interest in all elections'.

Even though he was never chairman or even a trustee, Robert Dickinson is generally regarded as the founder of the Rock. For the first 12 years, it is

John Mawson, first chairman of Northern Counties. Like many of his successors he played a distinguished part in the politics and business of the north-east. He was to die tragically not long after becoming Sheriff of the City of Newcastle.

Clayton Street, *c.*1900. The Rock Building Society held its first meeting in Mr Bell's temperance hotel in West Clayton Street, January 1865.

Facing page: Whitley Bay. Northern Counties and Rock agencies opened soon in many parts of the region, particularly on the coast.

true all the society's business was conducted from his office at 64 Pilgrim Street where, in 1862, the 26-year-old Robert had set up practice as a solicitor. And his great-grandson believes that one of his motives for taking up the Rock was the conveyancing business that building society work would bring. But oddly, in a memoir written by his son, also called Robert, his work with the Rock is not mentioned.

Unlike his fellow directors, Dickinson was a man of the prosperous outer suburbs. From the time of his marriage, he lived at Rose Villa, Gosforth, which, in the 1860s, was still known as Bulman's Village after a developer of 40-shilling freeholds called Job Bulman of Coxlodge Hall. In those days, Gosforth was much favoured by the ironmasters, shipbuilders, and other magnates who celebrated their success by building large villas in what was then the country. As there was, as yet, no public transport, Dickinson used to walk every morning from Gosforth to his Pilgrim Street office in the company of his great friend, Richard Welford, the writer, whose essays on leading figures in the region were published under the title *Men of Mark – Twixt Tyne and Tees*.

The Rock was set up on very similar lines to Northern Counties. And although the Tynesiders must by now have been quite familiar with the principles along which building societies were organised, the directors of the Rock plainly thought it would do no harm to restate them – simply and to the point. In a circular issued just three weeks after its foundation, under the heading 'Principles and Advantages of this Society', the Rock wrote:

> Experience has abundantly proved that Building Societies have been more successful in promoting the material welfare of those who avail themselves of the advantages they offer, than of any other of the various institutions having the same provident object in view.
> The advantages are twofold, namely – to afford a safe and profitable investment, and to enable persons of limited means to become owners, instead of mere occupiers, of their own dwellinghouse. No institutions combine the two great requirements of a good investment (namely perfect security and a high rate of interest) in the same degree as Building Societies.

The society got off to a most encouraging start. Within the first five weeks, subscribers had taken up shares worth a total of £13,830 and the society had agreed to pay out £2,715 in mortgage loans. By the end of the first year the Rock had eighty-nine shareholding members with 261 shares between them of which 138¼ had been advanced. Total assets were £8,687 10*s*.

Like the Northern Counties, the Rock's shares had a guaranteed value of £120 which were available in fractions of ½ and ¼ i.e. £60 and £30. The entrance fee was 2s. 6d. and subscriptions were payable monthly at 10s. per share. At the end of its first year, the society, after allowing for interest at 5 per cent compound, was in surplus to the tune of £181 1s. 11d.

In its very first year, the Rock opened a branch at Blaydon, a few miles west of the city, with its own local board of management and stewards. Already, the gaze of the Rock and Newcastle's other building societies was moving away from the city centre and its immediate surroundings towards the more enticing prospects to the north, east and west of the city. By 1865, the population of Newcastle had increased by a half in no more than 20 years and had now reached 122,000.

The first thrust was westwards into Elswick and Westgate as people moved closer to the shipyards and the engineering works that were springing up along the river. According to Sidney Middlebrook, 'the earliest and thickest expansion was in Elswick and the lower part of the parish of Westgate, where housing struggled to keep pace with the remarkable growth of the Armstrong Works. Between 1851 and 1871, the population of Elswick jumped from 3,539 to 27,801 while in Westgate it rose from 16,447 to 24,177. And where the people came, the houses followed – in terraced row upon row.

Lord William Armstrong (*below left*) founder of the great works at Elswick. The power-house of engineering in the north-east, it generated a massive demand for housing. The 1970s aerial photograph (*below right*), taken by Professor Norman McCord, shows the tightly-packed housing built for Elswick workers – now mostly demolished.

The accelerating building boom and the rising income of the workers in the new factories sparked the building society explosion on Tyneside from 1851 onwards. As the first into the ring, Northern Counties was especially well placed to take advantage. Its annual reports for its first 15 years tell a story of uninterrupted growth and expansion. Their tone is one of surprised euphoria. 'The Directors . . . rejoice,' it said in reporting the results for 1865, 'that they are enabled again to congratulate the Members upon the steady, continuous, and satisfactory progress of the Society.'

However happy the directors may have been at the progress the society was making, they were soon to be cast into the deepest gloom by a human tragedy that was as dramatic as it was unexpected. At the age of 52, John Mawson was at the height of his career. His business was well established, his money troubles were over, and, as well as being chairman of the Northern Counties, he had recently been appointed Sheriff of Newcastle.

But on 17 December 1867, came disaster. He was sitting at lunch in a hotel in Grey Street when he was called out to see the acting chief constable and a Mr Spark who told him that there were currently nine canisters of nitroglycerine in an office in the Town Hall and that the town clerk was insisting that they be moved immediately. It seems that the explosives had been stored in the cellar of the White Lion, but when the new landlord discovered what they were, he quite literally dumped the problem on the town hall. The police needed the Sheriff's advice. Mawson decided that the best thing to do was to hire a horse and cart and take the canisters to the Town Moor and pour their contents down a disused pit shaft at the old Spital Tongues colliery. At first, the operation went well enough. All nine canisters had been already tipped into a deep gully, when Mawson decided that three of them, which were still suspiciously heavy, should be buried a small distance away. Apparently some of the nitroglycerine had crystallised inside the containers which were, therefore, still very volatile.

During this operation it seems that one of workmen dropped one of canisters on to the other two. The noise of the explosion was heard 15 miles away. The five people closest were killed instantly: Mawson and the town clerk who were watching a few yards away, escaped the full force of the blast. But they were, nonetheless, mortally injured. Mawson died two and a half days later, shortly before 3 a.m. on 19 December 1867.

Newcastle buried him with full civic honours. The town was dressed in black, and church bells were muffled. On the day of his death, the directors of the Northern Counties passed a motion expressing condolence to his widow and family on their sad misfortune and agreed that the entire board should attend his internment. On the very same day, Joseph Davison, a grocer and, as we have seen, one of the original moving spirits in the Land Society, was voted as

64 Pilgrim Street, the address of the Rock's first office, 1862–74.

100-ton gun – at that time the largest in the world – made at Elswick Works in 1876.

THE EXPLOSION ON THE TOWN MOOR, NEWCASTLE.

(From the *Monthly Chronicle* for March, 1888.)

Twenty years ago, a terrible accident occurred on the Town Moor, resulting in the deaths of eight persons, two of them esteemed and prominent citizens of Newcastle. Not since the Gateshead explosion had anything happened which startled and shocked the town so much as this singular and remarkable fatality. The story will not take long in the telling.

In December, 1867, the attention of the police was called to the fact that a quantity of explosive material was stored in a cellar in the White Hart Yard, Newcastle. On examination this proved to be nitro-glycerine, a compound produced by the action of a mixture of strong nitric and sulphuric acids on glycerine at low

A later newspaper account of the explosion at the Town Moor (*main picture*) which killed John Mawson and several of his companions.

his successor. It was thus left to Davison, who was to serve the society as chairman for the next 27 years, to consolidate the Northern Counties' enviable reputation as the leading building society in the north-east.

The society was already looking to extend its activities far beyond Newcastle. In March 1866, the board approved an additional loan to a Thomas Brown of Glasgow who had asked for an additional advance of forty-five shares for the development of six shops and seventy-four rooms. This deal indicates the society's growing self-confidence. Not only was it willing to lend outside its home patch, but in advancing quite large sums of money on commercial property, it was taking a significant step away from Mount Pleasant and its modest homeowners. Already smaller societies were beginning to look to the Northern Counties for support and shelter. In August 1866, the year before John Mawson's death, the Great Northern Society had asked if it could join forces.

However, the event that was to propel the Northern Counties into the limelight on the national stage took the society completely by surprise. In November 1868, a certain Mr Laing challenged the legality of the Northern Counties' rule that allowed it to borrow money at up to 5 per cent, provided the loans did not exceed two-thirds of the total amount secured on mortgage. Though it may sound like an abstruse technicality, to the Northern Counties (and many other northern building societies) the case raised an extremely important issue: namely, the society's freedom to borrow. This was already under attack from the Registrar of Friendly Societies, the splendidly named Tidd Pratt, who saw it as his duty to stop building societies from encroaching into the territory occupied by the

banks. The authorities were also, quite rightly, worried that if ambitious building societies borrowed too enthusiastically and too indiscriminately, they would not only endanger their own stability, but that of their borrowers. There was too much at stake to risk any kind of building society melt-down.

As yet, the Registrar had not issued a definitive ukase. But if the court's decision went the wrong way, the consequences for the Northern Counties which, as we have seen, relied on loans from private investors like William Harle to kick-start its expansion, would be serious. The board waxed most indignant. At a special meeting at the Temperance Hall in Nelson Street in May 1869, the directors expressed their astonishment that a suit had been brought against them in the Chancery Division, and strongly refuted Mr Laing's assertion that he was acting in the members' interests.

All, however, turned out well. After nearly a year, the Lord Chancellor, sitting with Lord Justice Giffard, pronounced in favour of the society, even though the Law Lords made it very clear that the society's power to borrow was most definitely circumscribed. The Lord Chancellor said: 'If the rule had authorised the trustees to raise an unlimited sum of money wholly regardless of the contributions which might be made by the members, that no doubt would be contrary to the interest and scope of the Act.'

The directors were delighted, even though it had cost the society £438 7s. 7d. to defend the action – the money being deducted from surplus profits. At a board meeting in November 1869, they voted to give 'cordial thanks to the Solicitors of the Society for the great attention and ability in the management of the defence in the Chancery Suit on behalf of the Trustees and for the successful termination of the suit before the Lord Chancellor and Lord Justice Giffard. They resolved to take supper together on an early day, that the Directors and officials of the Newcastle Building Society be invited to join, the expense to be defrayed by the persons attending'. In the annual report for 1869, the directors said: 'The effect of this decision will be to strengthen and confirm the previous stability of the Society and qualify it for more extensive business.'

On the eve of its twentieth anniversary, in December 1870, the decision was taken to move the office to 2 Market Street at a rent 'not exceeding £75 a year'. It was the beginning of an association with Market Street that has lasted to this day.

It is perhaps worth pausing for a moment to take stock. At its inception in 1850, the number of shares taken up numbered 305 $^4/_5$ and the income amounted to £2,295. Twenty years later, the number of shares issued had risen more than tenfold to 4,011 $^1/_5$ and income from subscriptions had risen equally to £24,691 6s. 10d. The secretary's salary was £218 19s. 4d.; the treasurer was paid £18 15s. and trustees' and directors' fees came to £33 15s. Clearly nobody was making a fortune out of working for the Northern Counties. The secretary and the treasurer were still part-time, the business only employed a couple of clerks, and, for the directors, the business was

An ever more prosperous middle class created a rapidly expanding demand for goods, houses – and leisure time, like this Victorian group on the north-east coast . . .

The Building Society Act of 1874, of Disraeli's Tory government, set the basic guidelines for the operation of the industry to this day.

still very much a sideline. But what was most gratifying, for both directors and members, was that the surplus had risen from £18 to £4,568 4s. 4d. This grand sum was testament to two decades of good husbandry and careful management by Charles Burney, the secretary.

The society's legal victory in London had consequences that reached far beyond Tyneside. When Prime Minister Disraeli's incoming Tory government came to draw up its 1874 Building Society Act which laid down the framework within which, broadly speaking, they have operated ever since, it used the Northern Counties' two-thirds-of-mortgage-assets rule to define the borrowing powers of the building societies. In this fashion, the Northern Counties made its first (if rather unexpected) bow on the national stage.

The debate over borrowing powers had one immediate effect: it concentrated the directors' minds on the practical consequences of their victory. In some ways, it was not a victory at all. The emphasis placed on the rigid two-thirds limit denied the society much-needed flexibility. But was there any way round this problem? The answer was the preference share – which was approved by shareholders at the twenty-first annual meeting on 21 January 1872. As its name suggests, the preference share offered investors greater security, ranking below deposits but above the normal subscription share.

It was the societies in the north-east who were among the first to introduce this new saving instrument. For example, preference shares were a feature of the Rock's operations from the outset, even though the society itself was much smaller. In the annual report for 1872, the Northern Counties' chairman, Joseph Davison, explained the board's thinking. He wrote:

Sanguine anticipations formed at the commencement of the year have, to a large extent, been realised, the number of shares taken up and the amount advanced being considerably in excess of any previous year, and these would have been still further increased, but the Directors have reluctantly been compelled to curtail the Society's business *in consequence of the rules limiting the amount of loans* [my italics].

It is perhaps no accident that in the next sentence but one, the chairman announced that the treasurer's salary was to be increased from £25 a year to £50 a year and that he would be required to attend the society's office every Monday, Wednesday and Saturday from 12 noon to 1 p.m. Managing the society's money was still very much a part-time job, but the introduction of preference and paid-up shares (the latter being a full value share available to non-subscribers) was a watershed in building society history. By creating a lump-sum investment pure and simple with no direct connection with house purchase or home ownership, it marks a definitive break with old terminating society tradition and ushers in the age of the modern two-tier building society. And by placing as much, if not more, emphasis on the building society as a home for savings rather than saving for a home, it reinforces the middle-class bias that was inherent in the movement from the outset.

As the Building Societies Commission observed in a report the previous year:

> The most remarkable features . . . are first the growth of the permanent societies; second the growth of the loan or deposit system . . . It is admitted by even an adverse witness that on the whole permanent societies have been as yet judiciously managed; that failures of building societies which used to be very frequent in the epoch of terminating societies alone, are now rare. It is, however, alleged that the growth of them has altogether changed the character . . . of the building society movement; that it tends to throw . . . [them] more and more . . . into the hands of the middle classes and secure for them its benefits.

In June 1874, there was a changing of the guard. In that month Charles Burney, who had been involved from the very beginning, died. In a letter of condolence written to his widow, Joseph Davison, the chairman, wrote:

> I have been requested by the Trustees and Directors of the Northern Counties Building Society to tender on their behalf an expression of deep and respectful sympathy under the heavy bereavement which you have suffered.

. . . but the majority of the population still had to scrape a living, like this Newcastle street trader (Grey's Monument in the background).

Coal, and ships to carry it, remained at the centre of industry. On the left, two collier brigantines on the Wear.

Offering this assurance of our sincere participation in your great sorrow, we are painfully impressed with the inadequacy of any attempt on our part to alleviate it. It is my earnest hope that strength and assistance may be vouchsafed from a higher source.

I hope however that it may be consolatory to know that with us, with whom your husband laboured for so many years and also by the whole body of members of this Society, his memory is held in affectionate esteem, and that we and they will ever remember with respect the great ability and efficiency with which he discharged the duties of his office.

This letter was acknowledged by Charles Burney's nephew, Charles Burney Catnach, who was, the following month, appointed to succeed his uncle as secretary. He was to serve the society in this capacity for the next 55 years.

Catnach arrived at a significant point in the society's history. Five months later, just before Christmas 1874, the directors held a special meeting in the Temperance Hall, Nelson Street, asking members to approve their decision to incorporate under the new Building Society Act, legislation which had been welcomed by the five-year-old *Building Societies Gazette* as the movement's 'Magna Carta'.

Existing societies, like the Northern Counties, were under no compulsion to incorporate but those that did so, enjoyed a number of privileges. They became legal entities with limited liability and they could hold mortgage deeds themselves instead of through trustees. As we have seen, they were allowed to borrow up to two-thirds of their mortgage assets, but they were also required to be more accountable. They were prohibited from owning property, apart from their own offices. They had to make annual audits and statements of funds both to their members and to the Chief Registrar, though the £5 penalty for failing to do so could hardly be described as onerous.

The Act was not perfect. It contained a number of loopholes through which fraudulent promoters like Richard Benjamin Starr, creator of the Starr Bowkett societies, and Jabez Balfour, of the Liberator, would drive a coach and horses, but the new Act went a long way to putting building societies on to a businesslike footing. It also helped to create a new managerial class within building societies. In the larger societies, at least, the managers worked more or less full-time. Their professionalism and acumen were put to the test by the sudden collapse of English agriculture, the most serious economic setback for half a century.

In 1882 Newcastle became a city and St Nicholas's Church became a Cathedral. (In the 1990s Chris Sharp, Northern Rock chief executive, led an appeal to raise funds for new bells.)

Highbury and (*inset*) a contemporary photograph of the development of middle-income housing in Jesmond in the 1870s and 1880s.

4

The Flight to the Suburbs

The shock of the agricultural slump was all the greater for being so unexpected. For both Northern Counties and for the Rock, 1875 had been a record year. The building business was booming. In no more than three years, the number of houses built in Newcastle had nearly tripled – from around 4,000 in 1870 to over 11,000 in 1875. By the 1880s department stores, such as Bainbridge & Co. and Fenwick Ltd, had been established; the new Osborne Road cut through Jesmond, running northwards towards Gosforth; and new horse-drawn trams that were in time to connect the outlying districts of Gosforth, Elswick and Byker with the city centre were only four years away.

In February 1876, when the members of the Northern Counties gathered at Central Hall in Hood Street to celebrate the society's twenty-fifth anniversary, the mood was still upbeat. The outgoing trustees, Joseph Davison, W. B. Leighton, Mason Watson and Ralph Cook, were presented with elegant silver tea and coffee services from Listers in recognition of their services over the past quarter of a century; the secretary took the opportunity to remind the members of how the society's income had grown from £2,490 in 1851 to a present £248,601; and the evening concluded with some excellent songs and duets given by Miss Phillips, Miss Hall, Mr Stone, Mr Taylor and Mr Thwaites.

In the 10 years since its foundation the Rock, like the Northern Counties, had prospered. The first chairman, George Weatherhead, had been succeeded by Thomas Davis, a bank agent. But the secretary, Edward Lewins who also ran a stockbroking business under the name of Lewins & Co., was still there. By 1875, the Rock had 537 members who had invested very nearly £111,000 – almost double the total for the previous year – and had over £60,000 on loan to members. The Rock was still only

The demand for goods by rising middle-class affluence led to the arrival of department stores such as Fenwick Ltd and Bainbridge & Co.

The Rock moved to 76 Grey Street in 1875.

Grey Street, on Saturday morning was 'a parade ground for Jesmond's élite'.

half the size of the Northern Counties but the gap between them was beginning to close.

Spurred on by these encouraging results, the Rock moved out of Robert Dickinson's Pilgrim Street offices where it had started life to 76 Grey Street, next door to a high-class boot and shoemaker. Grey Street was already one of Newcastle's smarter shopping streets which included such well-known Newcastle names as Reids, jewellers, Listers and Davisons, both silversmiths, and Wilsons, woollen merchants. In a letter written when he was 91 to George Robson, the Rock's general manager, W. Graham, who joined the Rock as an office boy in 1889, described Grey Street on a Saturday morning as 'a parade ground for Jesmond's élite'.

But barely had the Rock settled in its smart new premises when the great depression struck. It was the countryside that was hardest hit. G. M. Trevelyan says in his Social History of England that in 10 years the acreage devoted to wheat fell by nearly a million acres and 100,000 farm labourers left the land. No longer protected by the Corn Laws, England's farmers suffered the full impact of American grain imports. And as agricultural incomes fell, the effect was quickly felt in the manufacturing towns and cities.

Newcastle did not escape. The building boom collapsed, and with it the demand for mortgages. In the space of five years, the Northern Counties' annual advances fell from £141,081 in 1875 to as low as £19,671 in 1880. At the Rock, the decline in mortgage demand was even more dramatic. From

The growth of new suburban housing had little impact on the large areas of decaying housing exemplified by this shot (*left*) of Tuthill Stairs in the 1880s.

The Great Depression of the late 1870s caused widespread hardship followed by industrial unrest. *Below*: 'On strike', by Hubert von Herkomer.

a peak of £61,892 in 1875, it fell right away to £5,594 – representing no more than 55 shares – in 1881. The mood of bright euphoria of a few years before had vanished completely. Building society managers' congenital tendency to always look on the bright side had been undermined by hard fact. 'In consequence of the severe depression existing in all branches of industry the Society's operations have . . . been somewhat restricted,' wrote the Rock chairman, Thomas Davis, in 1878. But in a brave attempt at optimism, he added: 'Notwithstanding this commercial depression, the Directors hope that with the assistance of each Member the progress hitherto made by the Society may in future be maintained.' However, it was not until 1882, that the clouds began to lift.

The clouds might have been very black, but there was also a bright shaft of sunlight. With money so cheap, and building society rates so attractive – they remained virtually unchanged at between 4½ per cent and 5 per cent throughout the second half of the nineteenth century – more money poured into the building societies than they knew what to do with. The obvious

In Jesmond, fine houses like this mansion in Lindisfarne Road, were followed by more modest terraced houses, such as those illustrated at the beginning of the chapter.

A familiar scene, no doubt, in homes like the one above.

course would have been to cut the rate to investors, but many societies were prevented by their own archaic rules from doing so. This did not apply to the Rock which in 1881, with advances plummeting to a new low, decided to cut the rate on its preference shares from 5 to 4½ per cent. The new chairman, Thomas Forsyth, one of the city's most active builders and property developers, told members: 'Even at this reduced rate of interest, money is very plentiful, and if an increase in the number of securities can be obtained, the business of the Society can be most profitably extended.' The paradox of the Great Depression as far as building societies were concerned was that although the level of activity may have been very low – it took the Northern Counties 44 years to return to the 1875 level of lending – building society balance sheets were never stronger.

The only way an honest building society could wander off the straight path of prudence and financial rectitude, was to be tempted to boost business by lending unwisely. This was naturally not a course of action that ever crossed the mind of the men who ran the Northern Counties and the Rock. From the outset, their watchword was safety. They were cautious in their valuations, and conservative about the type of property on which they would lend – for its first 50 years the Rock did not lend on farms, shops or factories. Despite their origins and a great deal of rhetoric about the moral and financial benefits of home-ownership, the vast proportion of the money lent by building societies did not go to owner-occupiers. And for one very good reason. There were very few of them. The most reliable authorities have calculated that prior to the First World War, the proportion of owner-occupied homes in England was not much more than 10 per cent of the total.

The vast majority of the Victorians and the Edwardians lived in private rented accommodation. Throughout the second half of the nineteenth century, the building societies' main customers were tradesmen and professional people who invested in property as a nest egg – or to provide a useful second income. They also provided working capital for the small builders who were changing the face of the Victorian city.

The minutes of the Northern Counties provide ample evidence of this. Mostly the money was borrowed to buy half a dozen terraced houses at £250 apiece. Sometimes, the deals were bigger. On 7 September 1882 an application was received from the builder, William Temple, for an advance of £29,000 in respect of no fewer than seventy properties in Osborne Avenue, Holly Avenue and Bryon Street. The survey committee reported that the value of the property was such as to warrant them recommending the application to the board. In passing it was noted that William Temple was a director of the society.

William Temple was not the only builder on the Rock's board. Thomas Forsyth, the chairman from 1880 until his death in 1905, ran Elswick Marble and Joinery from works at the back of Northumberland Street. With his brother, James, who was also a Rock director, Thomas was the man who brought the so-called 'Tyneside flat' to West Jesmond, an area of large

Fenwick Ltd today.

Left: Osborne Terrace, Jesmond, *c.* 1910.

Below: the demand for sophisticated domestic apparatus was inexhaustible.

Tyneside flats, photographed here in the 1970s, 'A valiant effort to squeeze a quart into a pint pot.'

Horsebuses, like these which ran to Gateshead, and horse-drawn trams, were gradually superseded by electric trams and trains, facilitating the expansion of the suburbs.

villas and distinctive terraced housing. As the big estates were sold off and broken up, the character of the district began to change as speculative builders like Temple and Forsyth moved in. One of the amenities of the big houses off the Osborne Road had been fine views across the Town Moor, but with the arrival of the developers, the area became less genteel and the views began to be obscured by unwelcome rows of terraced housing. It was an early example of the 'Nimby' (not in my back yard) syndrome that was to spread through the prosperous commuter villages of southern Britain about 100 years later.

At one to an acre, the Osborne villas were the homes of rich merchants and professionals. In 1880, the owners included a shipbuilder, timber and slate merchants, an earthenware manufacturer and a stationer. Osborne Avenue was inhabited by accountants, solicitors and a few merchants and builders. But it was just to the rest that the big changes came.

Here the Temples and the Forsyths put up rows of Tyneside flats for people several rungs lower down the social ladder than the grand folk along Osborne Avenue. The Tyneside flat was the result of Newcastle builders' ingenious efforts to cram as much housing on a single plot as possible while at the same time meeting the local authority's strict building regulations. In an effort to eradicate the worst excesses of speculative 'back-to-back' building, the authorities, from the 1850s onwards, had laid down minimum standards for street access, open space, windows, room heights, water supply, drainage and sewage. In essence, the Tyneside flat was a terraced house that had been divided horizontally into two. Its distinguishing feature was that it had two adjacent front doors, one leading to a ground-floor flat of three rooms, the other to an upstairs flat with four rooms. Both flats had sculleries and kitchen ranges and both had access, via separate staircases, to the backyard. It was, one might say, a valiant effort to squeeze a quart into a pint pot. And though the design never spread any distance beyond the banks of the Tyne, it seemed to serve Newcastle's and Gateshead's needs well enough.

As a one-off proposition, the Tyneside flat was never popular with the building societies. With

Dear Sir
At the Annual Meeting held on Monday
night Mr Goulden moved in eulogistic terms

Jabez Balfour. The crash of his Liberator Building Society in 1892 reverberated through the building society business.

two households occupying, as they saw it, a single building, they were worried about the ownership of the title. The societies' solicitors puzzled as to which householder would be responsible if it ever came to foreclosure. There were, however, no such problems about the flats when offered in bulk as security by the developer in return for a loan. When the Temples or the Forsyths applied for loans to finance the development of West Jesmond, the Rock was more than happy to oblige.

The change in the character of Jesmond began slowly. As late as 1890, 'the splendid suburb' was still, so Middlebrook says, 'exclusively occupied by handsome dwelling houses'. As a result the population rose only slowly. In the 40 years from 1851 to 1891 it rose from just over 2,000 to 8,400. The big jump came in the next ten years spanning the turn of the century. By 1911, the population had leapt to over 21,000. Jesmond fanned out from the upper part of the Osborne Road. It thrust across the railway towards the edge of the Moor in one direction, and it filled the space between Grosvenor Road and Osborne Avenue in the other.

By 1914 the long strings of streets of two-flat dwellings between St George's Terrace and Highbury had been completed and Osborne Road, built up now to the very top had made contact with Bulman's Village through High West Jesmond. By 1901, the horse-drawn trams had been replaced by electric trams. But the motor car was still almost unknown.

As the nineteenth century entered its last decade, confidence in the building society movement was badly shaken by the crash in 1892 of Balfour's Liberator, the country's third largest building society, and the near-failure of the Birbeck which was more of a bank than a building society. It was saved from immediate collapse by the Bank of England but eventually went under in 1911. Total building society assets fell by £10 million as investors throughout England voted with their wallets. In the south, the National Building Society saw its funds fall by over £500,000 between 1891 and 1897. In Newcastle, the effect of the Liberator affair was less marked. At the Northern Counties income peaked in 1891 at £121,000 before falling to a trough of £65,000 in 1897 – the year of Queen Victoria's Jubilee and the year of Newcastle's Great Industrial Exhibition.

By contrast, confidence in the Rock soared. In 1889, the society set a trend by negotiating an

An early electric commuter train which ran between Manors and Benton, stopping at Jesmond on the way.

The Rock moved from its cramped quarters in Grey Street to larger rooms at 59 Northumberland Street where it remained until 1910, when it moved to Market Street.

Northumberland Street, Newcastle on Tyne.

59 Northumberland Street today.

income tax deal with the Inland Revenue which foreshadowed the Revenue's own proposals five years later. From a record intake of funds of £27,316 in 1892, income rose sharply in 1897 to £43,199. Encouraged by these successes, in about 1895 the Rock moved from its cramped quarters in Grey Street to larger rooms at 59 Northumberland Street where it remained until 1910 when it finally arrived in Market Street. The premises were imposing. The picture on the front of that year's annual report shows a façade with four Ionic pillars flanking windows set on either side of the front door with the legend 'The Rock Permanent Building Society' elaborately engraved on the glass panel. Through the windows, the clerks had an excellent view of the Northern Counties, right across the street.

Some idea of the scope of the Rock's business at about this time can be gained from the fact that in 1899 of the 216 properties mortgaged, 140 were on property valued at £500 or less, fifty-six were worth between £500 and £1,000, sixteen were in the £1,000 to £3,000 bracket, two were in the £3,000 to £5,000 range and two were valued at over £5,000. Under Thomas Forsyth's leadership, the value of the Rock's assets had more than doubled in the last quarter of the nineteenth century – from £120,000 to just under £250,000. But growth in membership was much slower – from 425 in 1881 when Forsyth took over from Thomas Davis, to 547 when he died in 1905.

That they came through the 'Nervous Nineties' largely unscathed was a cause of much satisfaction on both sides of Market Street. At the Northern Counties, the last link with the founding generation had been broken with the death of Joseph Davison in February 1889. He had served the Northern Counties in various capacities for 38 years, including 21 as chairman. After stability, came a period of rapid change with three chairman in six years.

The first, Mason Watson, died within six months. The second, Edward Watson, who took up the post in May 1890, was a Newcastle man through and through. A lifelong Methodist, he was a scholar in the Sunday school of the old Bethlehem chapel when he was only five. A confirmed teetotaller at 14, he began in shipyards as an apprentice shipwright, spent 14 years in the corn trade, before changing tack in 1876 to become an estate agent. He set up business in the offices of his former employer, who had been so impressed by him that they presented him with all the office furniture as a gesture of goodwill. Later he took his son into partnership and between them they built up one of the largest and most successful estate agencies in the city. He was also a large property owner. He died suddenly from a heart attack in June 1895 just after he had addressed a Band of Hope demonstration at a Methodist conference in Halifax. He was succeeded by the powerful figure of Councillor Hugh Morton, JP.

Although Morton was a Scotsman by birth, he too had lived in Newcastle nearly all his life. He was a prosperous tailor and draper, who was destined to guide the society through some of the most eventful years of its history. He had a vigorous, no-nonsense style. Immediately after his election in July 1895, Morton set off to inspect some land the society owned in Stockton. A week or so later he reported to the board:

Edward Watson, chairman of Northern Counties, 1890 to 1895 - 'a Newcastle man through and through'.

In the Boer War Armstrong's Elswick Works raised a unit of gunners, photographed here in South Africa in 1901.

Above and facing page: contrasting life styles in the 1890s.

The electric tram extended the range of the suburban commuter.

Gentlemen – Our agent at Stockton (Mr Fletcher) having intimated to the Secretary that he had offers for certain of our properties there I went on the 7th of this month to consult with him thereon. The result I give herewith. For a plot of land at Thornby he submitted an offer which did not amount to more than 2*s.* per yard. I think this price is absolutely inadequate. We should get about 7*s.* per yard as it has a corner frontage. For a plot on Ewbanks estate at Stockton an offer was made of £125, rather less than 5*s.* per yard. I am of the opinion that we shall get at least 6*s.* per yard, that sum being no more than is obtained close at hand for building sites.

By the turn of the century, the Northern Counties had become unquestionably one of Newcastle's established institutions. When the society held its 50th anniversary Jubilee Dinner at the Grand Assembly Rooms, Barras Bridge (tickets 5*s.*, exclusive of wine) the guest list was a roll call of north-east's civic establishment. Amongst those invited were: the Mayor and Sheriff of Newcastle, the Mayor of Gateshead, the Under-Sheriff of Newcastle, the MPs for Newcastle, Gateshead and Tyneside, the Recorder of Newcastle, the Bishop of Newcastle, the chairmen and secretaries of the Newcastle, Grainger and Universal Building Societies, the presidents of the Law Society and Northern Architects Union, the chairman of the Tyne Commissioners, and the editors of the *Newcastle Journal,* the *Chronicle,* the *Leader* and the *Morning Mail.*

But if the Northern Counties was already well established in its home town, it was also nurturing national ambitions. The time had come to stand up for the regions – and especially the north-east. In May 1904, the board decided it would be a good idea if it invited the Building Societies

Association to hold its annual meeting in Newcastle as soon as practicable. It was left to the chairman and the secretary to make the arrangements.

The invitation was accepted. And almost exactly two years later, Newcastle was doing the BSA proud. The menu card for the official dinner was in green and gold with arms of the city – dragons, castles and lions prancing above the legend 'Fortiter Defendit Triumphans' – embossed in gold on the cover. Inside, the menu was decorated with pictures of the High-Level Bridge, the castle and the cathedral church of St Nicholas. After a feast of consomée paysanne, boiled salmon with hollandaise sauce, chicken cutlets, lamb with mint sauce, roast Aylesbury duckling, iced biscuits, dessert and black coffee, the company toasted the King, the Queen, the Prince and Princess of Wales, the clergy and ministers of all denominations, his Majesty's Imperial Forces, Success to the Building Societies Association, the Mayor, the Sheriff and Corporation of Newcastle, Success to the Newcastle Building Societies, the Visitors, the Chairman. The Northern Counties, as befitted the city's largest building society, was well placed. Hugh Morton was seated two places to the left of the BSA chairman while Charles Burney Catnach was at the extreme right-hand end of the top table, next to the Bishop of Newcastle. Both God and Mammon were well represented.

'Summer Afternoon Tea' by Thomas Barrett.

One of the highlights of the meeting was a paper by the secretary of the Northern Counties on 'The Building Society movement and its relation to the city of Newcastle.'

After pointing out that there were twenty-nine building societies with total assets of £2,330,452 in a city of 270,000 inhabitants, Catnach declared that the animating principles of all building societies 'should be that of security, and that everything else should be made in a measure subservient thereto'. Amongst the prime requirements were 'competent and trustworthy officials' and 'care, knowledge and experience in making valuations and advances'. He stressed the importance of calculating interest on a monthly basis; disposing of properties in possession promptly and only charging interest when earned. He paid tribute to the small band of men who started the Northern Counties whose names, he conceded, might mean little to the present generation. And he concluded by saying that 'among the many agencies at work during the past sixty years which go to making a free and independent community none has accomplished more than (our) movement'. Within ten years, as Tyneside prepared to go to war, his words were to acquire a new meaning.

5

Between the Wars

In February 1914, Charles Burney Catnach, the long-serving secretary of the Northern Counties, entered into negotiations with Messrs Lamb and Edge, the agents acting for the trustees of the Grainger estate, to take a 21-year lease on premises then occupied by Mr Small round the corner at 28 Pilgrim Street. The plan was to link the existing Market Street office with the new one in Pilgrim Street so that Northern Counties would occupy a commanding position on the corner of one of Newcastle's busiest intersections. After a brisk haggle over the length of lease – 'the trustees don't normally like leases longer than 14 years', the solicitors said – the deal was done. Six months later, Britain was at war.

Initially, the war seemed very far away. The society's auditor wrote to say that he had seen a letter from the County Fire Office which stated that properties within a radius of five miles of the coast had been insured against aircraft and bombardment risks and that the remainder of the properties mortgaged to the society had been insured against aircraft risk only. But as Newcastle was some 350 miles away from the conflict in northern France, no aircraft and no bombs came to trouble the insurance companies. Even so, the human cost was quickly felt in Newcastle, as it was throughout the country.

In May 1915, Alderman W. J. Sanderson, wrote to the secretary from Eastfield Hall, Warkworth, thanking his fellow directors for their sympathy on the death of his son. 'Our boy loved his profession and died the death he so often said he would like to do and this is our consolation,' he wrote stoically. Two years later, it was the secretary's turn when directors wrote to console him and his wife for the death of his son, 2nd Lieutenant J. Burney Catnach, who had died of his wounds in France. Two months previously, Charles Burney Catnach told the

Facing page: 'The Building of the Tyne Bridge' by O. R. Dickey.
Inset: the opening ceremony in 1928.

During men's absence at the front, 1914–18, many of their jobs were done by women. This further stimulated the demand for women's suffrage.

Above: suffragettes in Northumberland Street.

Below: women drivers at Armstrong Whitworth, 1916.

board that his health was, as he put it, 'unsatisfactory' and it was agreed that the finance committee should consider the position and report.

However great the personal tragedies, the impact on the building society movement itself was far less dramatic. The rise in bank rate to 10 per cent immediately after the outbreak of war, meant that the rates societies were paying their investors became uncompetitive almost overnight. A great deal of money was withdrawn from building society accounts to be invested in higher-yielding War Loan and other government securities. As one lawyer giving evidence to a government enquiry on rent control in 1915 put it:

I cannot think that anyone will be prepared to lend on mortgage at 4½ per cent when they can get 5½ per cent today from Treasury bonds, and well over 5 per cent from Consols . . . which is a thing they can call in and realise at a moment's notice.

But as house building and house buying also came to a virtual halt between 1914 and 1918, the societies emerged from the war in good financial condition. The Northern Counties was virtually unscathed with total assets in 1918 only £40,000 down on the 1914 figure. The Rock was less fortunate. Its mortgage business collapsed – from £71,393 in 1914 to £12,474 by 1917. Quite why the wartime experiences of two, very similar societies working on opposite sides of the same street in central Newcastle should have been so very different is hard to fathom. But perhaps the absence of William George Turnbull, the Rock's dynamic general manager and secretary, had something to do with it. In 1916 Turnbull was called away on military service and did not return until 1919.

He had spent part of his childhood in Norway and, before becoming the Rock's secretary in 1912, he had been a partner in Messrs Gjemre & Co., a Newcastle firm of timber importers. According to George Robson, who filled the same posts between 1955 and 1964, it was Turnbull who transformed what had been a rather amateur and sleepy business into one that would challenge the Northern Counties for its title as Newcastle's leading building society. As Robson wrote: 'This remarkable man by his energy and zeal did much to extend the activities of the Society, and by taking advantage of the new thinking that was then arising as regards home ownership, was responsible for the remarkable growth of the Society which took place in the inter-war years.'

Newcastle schoolgirls presenting gifts to
soldiers on their way to the front.

Zeppelin raid on Elswick Works.

The Somme, in the closing stages, 1916. The battle gained the Allies just seven miles at the cost of over a million dead.

Turnbull may have been the architect of the Rock's striking success in the inter-war period, but the conditions for that success were, in large measure, created by the Asquith government in 1915. Concerned about the acute shortage of housing in the years immediately before the First World War and worried that private landlords would exploit the situation by driving up rents, the government passed the Increase of Rent and Mortgage Interest (War Restrictions) Act. The act imposed a 'rent freeze' for the duration of the war and for six months thereafter. Two years later, in 1917, the coalition government began to lay plans for a nationwide scheme of public housing subsidised by government and built by local authorities. And although the government subsidy was cancelled at the insistence of the Treasury shortly after the war, the local authority building programme helped to undermine the position of the private landlord.

Throughout the nineteenth century, it had been the private landlord, in partnership with the emerging building societies, who had financed the building of the Victorian family house. In 1914, nine out of ten British families still did not own their own home. The pre-war slump severely reduced the attractions of investing in property. But what effectively destroyed the private landlord and changed the face of the housing market was the 1915 Rent Act. Introduced as a temporary wartime measure, it became politically impossible to repeal at a time of rapid post-war inflation and acute housing shortage. As one writer has put it: 'Rent control in wartime transformed the pre-war slump into a capital levy on the small landlord. And the Tory champions of property did not rush, post-war, to salvage this most self-effacing of political interests.'

What happened in the period between the two World Wars changed the face of Britain and altered for ever the way people lived and thought about themselves. From 1919 onwards, the vast majority of houses built for rent were built by the local authorities. Nearly all private houses, on the other hand, were built by speculative builders for owner-occupiers and almost wholly financed by the building societies. The invention of the semi-detached house was for millions arguably the most important development of the twentieth century. The spread of the suburbs, encircling the old Victorian cities and reaching out into the countryside along the bypasses and the railway lines, indicated the degree to which the centre of gravity of British life had shifted. And in helping the new suburbanites to achieve their dream of *rus in urbe* the building societies not only ensured their own future but added enormously to general happiness and well-being. As John Burnett writes in his *Social History of Housing 1815–1970*:

Here was a great army of new recruits to the class, keenly anxious to demonstrate their arrival by the adoption of a life-style which separated them from the respectable poverty from which many of them had risen. To live in a new suburb rather than an old overcrowded town, in a detached or semi-detached villa rather than a back-to-back house, above all, to be able to buy a house instead of merely renting it, and to luxuriate in the sense of security and achievement which property-owning brought, were their predominant ambitions.

With victory over Germany in 1918 came a revival in confidence as demand for mortgages picked up strongly and savers returned to their old habits. On his return from the war, William Turnbull lost no time in putting new life into the Rock. He launched a marketing drive stressing the safety angle. The annual report for 1919 came with a red sticker on the cover which read: 'In cases where it is of vital necessity to have a sound investment for their money – and which never depreciates and no doubt of regular payment of interest half-yearly – there is no safer security obtainable than the ROCK PREFERENCE SHARES. It cannot be too strongly emphasised that IN THE ROCK one has A PERFECT SECURITY WITHOUT SHRINKAGE OF CAPITAL.' The beating of the drum had the desired effect. By 1923, as the society approached its fiftieth year, the directors of the Rock were congratulating themselves on their most successful year ever, with advances and mortgages topping the million pound mark.

Across the street at the Northern Counties, it was also boom time, although the pace was more sedate. In 1919 income rose by nearly one-third in a single year to just under £300,000 – the largest single increase in the society's history. The pressure of business was such that in November 1919 the board agreed that the surveyors who were finding it hard to visit all the outlying districts should have the use of a motor car for 'not more than two days each month'. By 1921, despite the coal strike, the society's assets had topped the £1 million mark for the first time and a typewriter made its appearance in the Market Street office. It was the end of inkwells and copperplate and the beginning of a era of cheap housing that ended only with the advent of the Second World War.

From the summer of 1920 onwards building costs went into free fall – down from over £1 per square foot to 9s. 4d. in under two years. And as costs fell, so did house prices. Neville Chamberlain's 1923 Housing Act, which offered a subsidy to private builders, gave the market a boost and lowered prices still further. In the outer London suburbs a three-bedroomed, two reception semi could be had for as little as £395 freehold in 1932 while houses on the new estates that were being constructed by builders like William Leech in Newcastle's hinterland were, at £280 leasehold, even

Labour saving devices and technologies started to become widely available as a result of mass production: typewriters in offices, gas cookers in homes and cars on the road.

Miners at Mounsett Fell, during the 1926 General Strike, digging coal for old people.

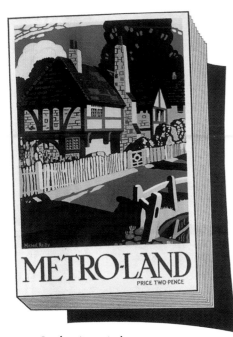

METRO·LAND
PRICE TWO·PENCE

London, in particular, saw a massive expansion of its suburbs in the 1930s, exemplified by 'Metroland', the term invented by the Metropolitan Railway.

The Northern Counties premises in Market Street, late 1920s. Rock expanded their premises opposite, at number 10.

cheaper. Northern Counties played a key role in Leech's business. Leech, whose methods were somewhat rough and ready, would build houses street by street. As each was completed – and sometimes even before it was completed – he would apply for a mortgage on behalf of the person to whom he just sold the house. He would then charge the owner a small sum, say £5 a month, and take out a second charge on his sale. The only problem was that not only did he fail to register this transaction but he also omitted to notify the building society of the change of ownership.

What made the houses even more affordable, were low interest rates – in the mid-1930s they fell below 5 per cent for the first time in building society history – and the willingness of Newcastle building societies to advance 80 or even 90 per cent of a loan. For the first time since the very early days of the land societies, well-built, comfortable housing was within reach of the ordinary wage-earner. The building societies had long served the housing needs of the professional classes; but now their clientele had changed and with new men came a new, more populist approach.

Once again it was William Turnbull's Rock that led the way. In the first five years after the war membership doubled; in the next five it doubled again to reach an impressive 14,196. In 10 years, membership of the Rock had risen tenfold. With its new Home Safe investor account, the Rock was aiming its sights directly at the small wage-earner and – significantly – his children. In a section of the annual report entitled 'How Members can help increase the popularity of the Rock' readers were advised to 'Talk 'Rock' with all your friends and invite them to support it with their savings . . . Encourage the kiddies to save their pennies – a penny a day – sixpence a week – may be safely put by and increases to an amount that is astonishing to anyone who has not studied the figures.'

A year later, in 1929, the Rock expanded its presence in Market Street by taking a lease on the shop next door at number 10. The directors of the Northern Counties could now look across the street at a classic façade with five window bays and an imposing double doorway. It was in that depression year that the Rock, after snapping at the Northern Counties' heels for the past 10 years, succeeded in overtaking its more staid rival by posting total assets of £2 million – a target that Northern Counties was not to reach until 1931. Having ruled the building society roost in Newcastle for so long, the Northern Counties fell to third place, behind the Rock and the Newcastle Building Society.

In September 1930 a young man called Arthur Rule joined the Northern Counties as an office junior. At that time, the society employed twelve people, a secretary, a managing clerk, a chief cashier, an accountant, five male clerks, two female clerks and the 16-year-old Arthur. The office walls and the counter were panelled in mahogany. There were four stations, each with a sloping desk with stained-glass fronts and individual lights. The desks were high and sloping with brass brackets on which to rest books and the clerks sat on high stools with no backs. The windows were narrow and the lower half of each was acid blasted. Because of its sombre outside appearance and elaborately decorated glass windows, the office got quite a number of callers who dropped in under the impression it was a pub. Rule's salary was 12*s*. a week and his duties reflected this modest wage. As he remembers almost 70 years later:

> I'd been told to report at 0830 hours in order to have everything ready for the staff when they arrived . . . It being a Monday this involved winding the office clock . . . filling the counter inkwells, changing the pen nibs (two pens to each inkwell -- one a relief nib and the other a ball point nib) and renew the blotting paper at each section of the counter . . . Next it was down to the basement to check on coal and coke stocks and rake and stoke the boiler. This had to be done several times per day as well as seeing to the coal fire in the boardroom. Woe betide you if you let them go out.
>
> As this was a very busy corner for traffic it was obviously considered necessary to have a boy to change the points for the tramcars. The office entrance was a convenient place for him to shelter but as these boys were constantly changing we had to ask them to stop banging their metal rod on the marble floor in the entrance lobby as it could be very disconcerting.
>
> Tea breaks were unheard of and smoking was forbidden. I well remember having to prepare a 'No Smoking' notice for display on the one and only respectable toilet (there was another in the basement but it was in a terrible state with fungus growing up the walls) as Mr Ross (the secretary) had followed someone in who had taken the opportunity of having a quick cigarette.

As it happened Arthur Rule had joined the Northern Counties at an historic moment. Just three months before, Charles Burney Catnach had retired after 55 years as secretary to the society. And just under a year after Rule's arrival, Hugh Morton was dead. He had been a director for half a century and chairman for 38 years.

With Charles Burney Catnach's retirement at the age of 77, the last link with the heroic and, by now, very distant past had been broken. In recognition of his exceptional service he had been appointed a director two years earlier – a signal honour as in the building society world even senior NCOs rarely joined the officer class. When the time came to stand down, he seemed lost for words. The

North East Coast Exhibition, 1929, was a determined attempt to boost the economy of the region.

Benwell Hall, home of William Bramble, chairman of Northern Counties from 1931 to 1946.

minutes record that: 'Mr Catnach feelingly referred to his long period of service and to the fact that he had attended every Annual Meeting since his appointment as Secretary 55 years ago, and he expressed how much he appreciated the kindness and consideration which had always been extended to him.' The connection with the society was not broken as he remained a director until his death in 1941. His successor was James Adams Ross, a Presbyterian from Aberdeen and a lover of church music, who had been promoted from managing clerk. As the new secretary, the starting salary was £750 a year – £21,300 in modern money.

In the 1930s, the Northern Counties, like all building societies, was run in a strict hierarchical fashion. The next most senior managers, the chief assistant and the accountant, were paid little more than half what the secretary earned; there was a ceiling of £200 a year for female clerks; and the pay for juniors and typists was wretched. In 1936 a typist with two years' service was earning £62 a year, while the office junior received £40. Few people went into the building society movement for the money. Compared to the banks, the wages and the status were low. For the clerical staff, the work may have been routine and dull. As there were no addressing machines, twice a year the two office juniors had to hand address all the envelopes sent to shareholders. This took so long that no sooner was one lot finished, than work started on the next. And the only way of keeping up with changes of address was to destroy the old envelope and write out a new one. But in the 1930s regular jobs of any kind were hard to come by and job security was good. Only if you were caught with your hand in the till, as some occasionally were, did you risk being fired.

In October 1931, Alderman William Bramble was appointed as the new chairman. An old school liberal, he was a man of parts. According to legend, he had walked on foot from Bishop Auckland, where he had been an apprentice bootmaker. With his possessions in a bundle on his back, he had arrived in Newcastle to seek his fortune. Like Dick Whittington, Bramble not only made his fortune, but became Lord Mayor of the city. In his later years, Bramble devoted much time to collecting rare books and researching local history. He wrote an excellent paper on the early years of the building society movement in the north-east which showed great sympathy for the poor and dispossessed. Bramble lived in some style in Benwell Hall where visitors had to call at the lodge before being admitted. There was then another wait at the front door for the dogs to be locked up. Apart from his books – he had a copy of every directory of Newcastle ever published – Bramble had a wonderful collection of grandfather clocks which he loved to show off by closing the shutters and lighting the gas mantles of the large room in which they were kept.

Bramble took over at a difficult time. The economy was in deep depression, and unemployment, especially on Tyneside was widespread. It was from the Jarrow shipyards that the marchers set to off for London to draw attention to their plight. In October 1931, only days after Bramble had taken office, came the election of the national government. The following June, bank rate was cut to 2 per cent. The aim was to stimulate production and to persuade holders of £2 billion worth of undated 5 per cent War Loan to convert to a new 3½ per cent issue.

Alderman William Bramble, here with his family. Like many Northern Counties and Rock chairmen, he was a leading figure in the north-east and became Lord Mayor of Newcastle.

The great Jarrow March, in protest at high unemployment, arrives in London.

The effect on the building societies, which were still offering 4 per cent tax free, was immediate: the flood of cash was so overwhelming that they were forced to ration new investments.

By 1933, the Northern Counties was turning away investors in large numbers. 'Financial conditions throughout the year were most uncertain and the continued cheapness of money attracted to Building Societies a large amount of money which was not of the nature of a permanent Building Society investment,' the directors reported. At the same time, the society was refusing mortgage applicants whose security, it claimed, was not good enough. The societies may have been keeping a close eye on their own affairs, but they were watching their rivals just as keenly.

To the alarm of the Building Societies Association, they started to compete vigorously between themselves. The BSA chairman, Enoch Hill, told the annual conference in 1933:

> In my long experience, I have not seen previously anything approaching the degree of competition, often regardless of courtesy as between one society and another, which has been experienced in the past year.

And he raised the quite shocking prospect of a price war.

> If this continues there will be no alternative but that every society should be free to adopt measures . . . to guard against a deflection of long associated business by undercutting terms.

'Hiking' by J. W. Tucker. The enjoyment of outdoor pursuits was widespread in the 1930s.

In the autumn of 1934, the BSA wrote to all its members to try and bring things under control. It suggested that no society should offer more than an 80 per cent advance for houses costing more than £500; that interest charged should be no less than 5 per cent; and that the maximum rate for new investors should be fixed at 3 per cent. It also deprecated the practice of paying commission to agents for introducing business. All this did not go down well with the Northern Counties. James Ross replied stiffly that the society had always lent at 90 per cent of valuation; that it never paid for the introduction of mortgage business; and that 'attention seems to have been paid principally to the desires and requirements of the Societies in the London area.' Ross concluded with a robust defence of northern ways. 'The board was', he said, 'of the opinion that some of the proposals interfere unduly with

The Rock office, Market Street, early 1930s.

the autonomy and self-governing powers of individual Societies, without due regard to the varying and long-established usages and practices in different areas of the country.'

There is an irony here. As an influential member of the local building society cartel, the Northumberland and Durham Building Societies Association, the Northern Counties had always been quick to act when its rivals in the area threatened to step out of line. But it was not going to be pushed about by the big boys in the south.

The strange thing was that while secretary Ross was protesting that the Northern Counties never paid anyone a commission, the records show the society hiring small town estate agents, accountants and solicitors as commission agents. When James Ross wrote his letter to the BSA, the society already had a chartered accountant in Hexham and an estate agent in Whitley Bay on the books. In Hexham, it was agreed that the agent was to be paid £25 for the first £2,500 of mortgage business; £56.25 for the next slice and so on up the scale. It was the beginning of a whole network of agents throughout the towns and villages of County Durham and Northumberland that would drive the next stage of the Newcastle building societies' expansion – a development that came to an abrupt, though temporary, halt in 1939.

6

Wider Horizons

As war approached in the summer of 1939, the directors of both the Northern Counties and the Rock began to worry about security. The papers were full of stories of enemy air raids and the damage they might do if or, as most people expected, when war broke out. Both societies were concerned that if Market Street was hit, mortgage deeds worth several million pounds would be destroyed. Consequently in May 1939, the board of Northern Counties asked for a report on the strong room. A month later, the directors were told it might be a good idea to strengthen the roof. The estimate for the work came to £15. The board also asked the secretary to investigate alternative accommodation in the country, but nothing came of this and Northern Counties stayed put.

The Rock, advised that its strongroom would not withstand an air raid, decided on a more drastic course. Shortly before war broke out, all the deeds, together with the mortgage and investment departments, were moved to 'Heatherlea', a former hotel in the remote village of Allendale, some 25 miles west of Newcastle, where they were to remain until November 1943. With one dissension, it was agreed those members of staff who were called up should continue to receive their full pay less army pay and allowances, and that because of the blackout, the office would open at 8.30 a.m. and close at 4 p.m. For the same reason, board meetings were rescheduled for noon.

As in 1914, the declaration of war against Nazi Germany was quickly followed by a short but very sharp outflow of funds. The reasons were different: money was expensive in 1914 and very cheap in 1939, but the results were very similar. In the early months of 1939, the outflow of money from both the Northern Counties and the Rock, as savers withdrew their deposits, reached alarming proportions. In two months, the Rock's overdraft

London branch office in Maddox Street, opened shortly after the Rock opened its first London branch at 17 Conduit Street.

Churchill visiting a Newcastle shipyard
during the Second World War.

Theory and the practice: emerging
from an Anderson shelter in
Newcastle after an air raid.

at the bank more than doubled from nearly £60,000 to close to £120,000, and at Northern Counties, the situation so frightened the 79-year-old Charles Burney Catnach that he put down a motion which noted: 'Inasmuch as we have no balance at the bank and are not receiving sufficient in Preference Shares to meet the current business, it is inadvisable to make future advance business at a lesser rate than 4¾ or 5 per cent.' But as the former secretary could find no one to second his motion, it was dropped.

In any case, it was a non-starter. In a weak market, the last thing anybody would want to do was to raise the cost of mortgages. In 1939, as in 1914, the demand for mortgages had fallen away to almost nothing. In August 1939, the Rock's solicitor told the board that in the past month just sixteen mortgages totalling £6,960 had been transacted. The low level of mortgage business lessened the strain on societies' cash flow. But the Northern Counties and Rock were not prepared to leave things to chance. Sheltering under the umbrella of the Northumberland and Durham Building Societies, they agreed to follow the example of the Yorkshire societies and cut the rate to investors from 3½ to 3 per cent – a move, so James Ross of Northern Counties calculated, would have a dramatic effect on the society's profit. He reckoned, on current turnover, it would rise from just under £3,000 to a whisker over £14,000. It says volumes for the patriotism of the Northern Counties' directors that at the very time when they were straining every nerve to woo back their investors, they were willing to invest £10,000 of the society's money in short-dated War Bonds paying just 2½ per cent.

However fearful the building societies may have been of enemy air raids, the north-east escaped comparatively lightly compared with cities like Coventry and Southampton and the east end of London. By the autumn of 1940, some fifty-five houses on mortgage to the Rock had suffered slight war damage, and the Northern Counties reported that up to the end of 1941, 249 of their buildings had been damaged and only eighteen had been totally destroyed.

Sharp though the liquidity crisis was, by 1942 things had improved so markedly that the Rock was obliged to limit new investments to £50. On 5 July 1942 Charles Burney Catnach died aged 82. In all, he had served the society, as office boy, secretary and director, for 62 years. When he joined the Northern Counties as an office boy aged 15, Gladstone had just completed his first term as prime minister. When he died, Queen Victoria had been dead for 40 years, he had outlasted two generations of Dickinsons at the Rock and narrowly missed the arrival of the third. As the chairman of the Northern Counties, William Bramble, observed: 'This long and continuous service must be unique in Building Society annals.' By general agreement, the vacancy on the board created by Catnach's death was not filled and the number of directors was reduced to ten.

In January 1943, five months after Catnach's death, there was an equally significant rite of passage at the Rock. There had been a vacancy on the board ever since the death of one of the directors, W. B. Nisbet, the previous October. Originally, there had been only one name, that of H. A. Haslam. Then Councillor Norman Chapman put forward his own nominee, H. J. Thompson. And finally, the name of Robert J. Dickinson, the society's solicitor, and grandson of the original Robert Dickinson, emerged. As the time for decision approached, the first two candidates withdrew, leaving the field to the solicitor. After a gap of 15 years (the second Robert Dickinson having died in 1928) there was once again a Dickinson on the Rock board.

In the 80 years or so that the Dickinsons had been practising law in Newcastle, the family and the practice – by now known as Dickinson, Miller and Turnbull – had flourished. The Dickinsons were an ambitious family with a shrewd, business-getting instinct. The first Robert had become involved with building societies as a means of increasing his conveyancing business; and the second Robert had swelled the family fortune by branching out into property development with the help of the Rock. But it was the third Robert, or Roy, as he was usually known, who formed a number of shrewd alliances, both business and personal, with the region's biggest landowners that was to put the family on an almost equal footing with his aristocratic clients.

Dickinson was one of those infuriating people who are dazzlingly successful at everything they turn their hands to. A brilliant athlete, he was president of athletics at Oxford, represented England as a high-jumper at the 1924 'Chariots of Fire' Paris Olympics and was also a very gifted law student who passed his Law Society exams and came top of the first-class honours list. He did not lack confidence in his abilities. When his father died shortly before he qualified, he announced to Turnbull, the remaining partner and brother of William George Turnbull, the former general manager of the Rock, that if he were to join the firm, he would do so only on the condition that he was the senior partner. Turnbull eventually agreed and sold his interest. Young Roy was therefore in

Top: munitions workers at Vickers Armstrong, 1940. Innumerable war jobs for women included the Land Army.

Devastation after an air raid on South Shields market-place, 1941.

Lord Matt Ridley, seen here in his racing car, would become the Rock's chairman in 1946.

Lord Ridley and two sons: left, Nicholas, later MP, and on the right the future 4th Viscount who would in his turn become chairman.

the somewhat curious, though not unpleasant, position of being the sole ruler of the family firm for his entire working life. His son says he was in no way an autocrat – just powerful. And he used that power to build the family business into the leading firm in Newcastle.

Dickinson was both energetic and able. But at the same time, his career was greatly helped, as his son acknowledges, by the fact that he married a Joicey. As a coal magnate and landowner on a grand scale, Lord Joicey was the perfect patron for a young and ambitious solicitor. Within a few years, not only was Dickinson, Miller and Turnbull handling all Lord Joicey's land trust business, it was doing similar work for other large landlords.

It was through the Joicey connection that Dickinson came to know the leading member of another coal-rich, landowning family with deep roots in the north-east, Lord Ridley. The owner of Blagdon, a 10,000-acre estate on the northern outskirts of Newcastle, Matt Ridley was, or at least gave the appearance of being, a throw-back to an earlier era when lords were not lords unless they were devoted to fast cars, high living and an insouciant eye for a well-turned ankle.

Born in 1902, Lord Ridley, who succeeded to the title when he was only 14, had a carefree youth. He went to Eton; was one of the Bright Young Things so brilliantly described by Evelyn Waugh in *Brideshead Revisited*; and though he was fond of the customary country sports, his big passion was motor cars. In the 1930s he built his own racing car with a top speed of 105 mph which he raced at Brooklands and broke a world speed record for 650 cc cars. At the wheel of his vintage Alfa Romeo, with his white hair and his long, fur-collared, racing-driver's coat, he was one of the sights of Newcastle.

There was, however, more to Matt Ridley than the portrait of this somewhat raffish figure suggests. The offhand, rather peremptory, aristocratic manner frightened some while concealing a sharp mind, a gift for organisation, and a fascination with and aptitude for technology that went far beyond that of a dilettante racing driver. His talents were first put to use during the war when he was the representative of Lord Beaverbrook's Ministry of Production in the north-east; a role he combined with building factories to manufacture gas for barrage balloons. He was chairman of Consett Iron, and was on the board of the LNER railway company. He was chairman of the council of Newcastle University from its inception, was twice chairman of Northumberland County Council and also served as chairman of the North-East Development Association. In February 1945 Matt Ridley would join the board of the Rock Building Society. Just over a year later, in March 1946, he had become chairman, following James Easten who joined the society in 1921 as a surveyor and had been chairman since 1935. Over the next 20 years, with his friend Roy Dickinson, Ridley was to give the Rock a renewed sense of purpose and direction.

Even before Lord Ridley's arrival, the anxiety and gloom of 1941 and 1942 had disappeared. Northern Counties and the Rock felt confident enough to plan for post-war years. Nor were they alone. In the summer of 1944, the directors of Northern Counties received a prescient letter from William Wetherill, the secretary of the Isle of Thanet Building Society. He wrote that his board 'had given much thought to the present trend among Building Societies towards amalgamation and the recent linking up of very large Societies.' And he suggested 'a scheme for grouping a number of societies on a local-regional basis so as to combine their strength whilst allowing them to retain their own identity and function to all intents and purposes as individual units.' He thought that the group should consist of seven societies from all parts of the country and he named the Marsden, Northern Counties, Leeds and Holbeck, Birmingham Incorporated, Bristol and West and Hearts of Oak. The idea was that the group would have comparable weight and mass to the Abbey or the Halifax, while preserving local identity and autonomy.

The Northern Counties rejected this ingenious idea on the grounds that it was its policy to confine its mortgage business to the four northern counties. James Ross replied that 'the question of amalgamation is being carefully watched by my Board but if any such proposition should be made they would prefer it should be by local Societies joining together.' This last point was not an academic one. In that very same year, the Northern Counties had made its first takeover for 91 years when it agreed a transfer of engagements with the Armstrong Permanent. Though nobody knew it at the time, the acquisition of the Armstrong was the beginning of a trend that would not only utterly change the character of the Northern Counties itself but would lead directly to the creation of Northern Rock and its subsequent emergence as one of Britain's top ten building societies.

While the Northern Counties was beginning to consolidate its grip over its own territory, the Rock was looking further afield. In February 1945, the board decided that the time had come to open a branch in Birmingham. This was a significant move on two counts: firstly it clearly showed that the Rock's horizons were wider than Northern Counties' and secondly it

Evening Chronicle and *Picture Post* victory editions.

Happy residents celebrate in Tamworth Street, Arthur's Hill, Newcastle.

New housing was a high priority
after the War.

Above: a new estate
in Newcastle, 1950s.

Below: high rise flats under
construction in Scotswood Road.

recognised the importance of a branch network as a means of building business. If the 1930s was the decade of the agent, then the 1950s was the age of the branch. Even so, the Rock was not going to ignore opportunities on its own doorstep. In April 1946, it matched the Northern Counties' move by acquiring a Newcastle building society for itself, the Prince of Wales Permanent Benefit. In themselves these acquisitions were not that significant: the societies were small and run mostly as a sideline by local solicitors and accountants. But what these deals did indicate was that after such a long period of stasis, when the number of Newcastle building societies seemed immutable, the ice was melting. From now on, it would be the survival of the fittest.

In a board paper written in May 1945 and entitled 'Post-War Finance of Housing', the Rock peered into the future. In contrast to the period immediately after the First World War, it saw a large role for the private sector. 'In the post-war period, it appears that the three sources (of housing) will be builders, local authorities and large employers of labour seeking to provide housing for their people. Government action may also be expected, but whatever form it may take, it appears probable that private enterprise will be called upon to fulfil the major part of the programme.' After saying that it was prepared to advance up to 95 per cent of the purchase price, the Rock said that it would help builders wishing to buy land for housing by lending them up to 80 per cent of the land's value and in some cases, it said, the amount advanced on the land would be regarded as part of the total to be advanced on the houses comprising the total estate. If the builders were in the vanguard of the post-war building boom, then the building societies were hard on their heels.

The Rock emerged from the war in excellent shape. With total assets of £4.2 million it had fifteen branch offices throughout the north-east and was represented in nearly forty towns and cities from Aberdeen to Penzance throughout England, Scotland and Wales. In 1950, the Rock moved its offices from 10–14 Market Street to 5–7 Market Street. After spending the comparatively large sum of £1,800 on equipment, fittings and furnishings, the Lord Mayor of Newcastle and Rock director, Alderman N. H. Chapman, performed the opening ceremony. The shine was removed from the new office when soon after a corporation bus crashed into it, causing £1,000 worth of damage. But while it was still being repaired, the Rock took what was for a northern society a truly bold step: it took a lease on an office in London, at 17 Conduit Street. Dickinson, Miller and Turnbull opened their London office in this building as a tenant of the Rock, their principal clients being the Rock and MEPC.

By the end of the 1950s television was just beginning its rise as the centrepiece of home leisure time.

Shipbuilding would continue to be a major industry in the north east for another decade. Here, a huge tanker under construction looms over a street in Wallsend.

Housing Minister Harold Macmillan reached an agreement with the building societies further to stimulate home ownership.

Innovative appliances and materials for the home, and leisure time, 1950s.

The London office was a Ridley initiative. He reasoned that if the Rock were to increase its mortgage business, it needed a presence in the massive London market. It could no longer rely on the north-east where business had gone rather flat. The move was well-timed. The previous year a Conservative government had been returned to power which was committed to build 300,000 houses a year of which more than half would be constructed for owner occupation by the private sector. Owner occupation received a further boost when the Minister of Housing, Harold Macmillan, reached an agreement with the building societies to guarantee advances of up to 95 per cent on houses valued at less than £2000 and built after 1918, and 90 per cent on any house of whatever age worth up to £2,500. These measures would have less effect in the north where, as we have seen, 90 per cent advances were commonplace but the impact on the housing market in the south was distinctly encouraging.

If Lord Ridley was the impetus behind the London move, the implementation was the work of Roy Dickinson. A stockbroker friend called Jim Scrimgeour had introduced him to MEPC, the huge property company, which owned 17 Conduit Street and generally helped the Rock around the unfamiliar London property scene. The link with MEPC proved fruitful for everyone. The Rock benefited from the advice of senior MEPC people who joined its London board while Roy Dickinson, who was a property developer in his own right, became a director of MEPC. Under the guidance of Ray Chapman, who was brought in from the Burnley Building Society which, small as it was, had an industry-wide reputation for good management, the London operation prospered in the 1960s to the point where it was writing about half the Rock's total mortgage business. On the other hand, it was less successful in attracting investment money.

While the Rock was looking southwards, the Northern Counties was seeking to put its own house in order. The Northern Counties had been part of the Newcastle commercial establishment for so long that its directors had become a little complacent. Ever since the Rock came to Market Street, Northern Counties had been rather snooty about the Rock. As a young man, Arthur Rule remembers being ticked off by the secretary, James Ross, for being so bold as to speak to someone from the Rock in the street. Also, the fact that William Bramble, who had been chairman for 15 years and a director since 1902, was elderly and in poor health, probably served to blunt the edge of the Northern Counties' attack. In fact, Bramble retired in 1946 and was succeeded by Edward Darnell. The society was extremely solid but more than a little ponderous.

where he commanded a detachment of Indian troops, and rose to be a major before he was 30. By the time he returned, a job as a pen-pusher with the Co-op no longer seemed so attractive. The Co-op, then in the throes of reorganisation, did its best to keep him. They offered him a job in Manchester and when that didn't appeal, he was posted to Northern Ireland where he met his wife Maureen. Even so, he was restless. And when a Newcastle solicitor called Leslie Muckle told him that the Northern Counties was looking for someone to succeed James Ross who was due to retire after half a century as secretary and general manager, Osborn was receptive. Muckle was terse and to the point. 'Good job, sleepy outfit, nice people,' was how he summed it up.

Osborn lost little time in making his way in Newcastle society. He was taken under the wing of fellow-Gunner, Col. Rob Mould-Graham, an accountant in civilian life who was later to be Lord Mayor of Newcastle and the first chairman of Northern Rock. Inevitably it was not long before Osborn joined the Union Club, the power centre of Newcastle's business life. Just a short walk (7 minutes by Osborn's calculation) from the Northern Counties' office on the corner of Market Street and Pilgrim Street, the club was the meeting place for the gentlemen businessmen of Quayside, lawyers, accountants and shipping people. Osborn spent a great deal of time on what today would be called 'networking'. It was at the Union Club that Osborn would hear what the other Newcastle building societies were up to; which were ripe for takeover and which might be a threat to his own ambitions. In January 1952 the office paid what was then the tidy sum of £840 for a 12 year-old Daimler. It was a clear sign that a new man was in charge and that things were about to change.

The first York branch at the address where it was opened by Northern Counties in 1952.

7

The Creation of Northern Rock

Even for someone as forceful as Osborn, it took time for things to happen. The first six or seven years when Osborn was learning whom he could and could not rely on must have been frustrating. But then quite out of the blue a letter arrived which put an entirely new complexion on things. In April 1957, Lord Ridley wrote to Campbell Allan, the Northern Counties chairman, suggesting that it might be a good idea if the Rock and the Northern Counties got together. Allan was quite plainly taken by surprise. So he stalled. 'For a number of reasons, which I will not enumerate here, it has not been easy to reach a conclusion as we wanted to avoid a hasty decision or a premature exchange of views,' he replied. 'There appears to be much to commend the idea of a union but the present is not a very convenient time for us to examine the matter. Could you leave the matter with me so that it may be examined more fully in a few months time?'

Over the next eight years the two societies danced a stately gavotte with both sides coyly taking turns to advance and retreat. In March 1959, the Northern Counties reopened negotiations, but by July they had again broken down. 'I think that we would have liked to have joined with you,' Lord Ridley wrote to Campbell Allan, 'had it been possible to work out various administrative matters which we discussed. It did seem, however, when we met these would be difficult to get over, and we accordingly came to the conclusion that we should reluctantly decide that the proposal should be abandoned.' Two years later, the new Northern Counties chairman, Col. Rob Mould-Graham met Lord Ridley to explore the same subject but with the same result.

There was very little to choose between the two societies in terms of size. As the housing market boomed in the late 1950s and early 1960s, both were growing at about the same rate – a healthy 8 per cent to 12 per cent a year.

Northern Rock House, Gosforth.

Left to right: the Bishop of Newcastle, with Campbell Allan, chairman of Northern Counties, and his successor Col. Rob Mould-Graham.

More signs of a rising standard of living in the 1950s.

Between 1953, when its London office in Conduit Street first opened its doors for business, and 1964, its anniversary year, the Rock's assets rose from £10 million to nearly £27 million. Over the same period, the Northern Counties grew from being an £8 million building society, to one with assets of some £32 million.

That the Northern Counties had managed to make up the ground it had lost to the Rock before the war and had succeeded once again in pushing its nose in front (if only just) reflects the vigorous leadership of Fuller Osborn. The Rock had progressed by nurturing its new London operation and by expanding its mortgage business with the assistance, among others, of William Leech, Newcastle's leading builder and developer.

Leech, who started as a window-cleaner, built himself up to be one of the biggest builders in the north-east, thanks in part to Roy Dickinson, who used to lend him £100 a week to help him pay the wages. Later Leech became one of Dickinson, Miller and Turnbull's largest clients, and from there it was a small and natural step to the Rock. As Leech's housebuilding business grew, he would deposit tens of thousands of pounds as collateral security for the mortgages the Rock was advancing to the buyers of his houses. This was good business for the Rock and good business for Leech, especially as the Rock was, for a long time, paying his company, Northern Homes and Estates Ltd., a commission on every mortgage it introduced.

Osborn's approach was rather less involved. As the Northern Counties had been slower off the mark than the Rock in building a branch network (it did not have a single branch until Osborn's arrival), Osborn decided that the most effective way of making up lost ground was to acquire as many other building societies as he possibly could. The man he chose to help him was Arthur Rule, whom he called his 'Man Friday'. Rule turned out to be ideally suited for the task. A stickler for detail, he played the part of the truffle hound to perfection. With dogged persistence, he would sniff out likely opportunities in the most unlikely places. In one instance, the society had set its sights on the Hebburn, which was run by the managing clerk of a local solicitor in the town. Unable to pin down either the secretary or the society's books, Rule was obliged to issue an ultimatum. Once found, he then marched the secretary home and turned everything upside down. Cheered on by the man's family and his grandchildren, Rule eventually found what he was looking for in boxes behind the piano, in drawers on the piano and in several other places besides.

One of Osborn's first targets was the Workington Building Society which proved elusive and was only captured at the third attempt. It was not until 1957 that Osborn scored his first hit when the Northern Counties gathered in the Crown, a Newcastle society almost as old as itself. Based in Eldon Square, the Crown was run by the Nixon family. The secretary was Isaac

Nixon, who was a friend of the Northern Counties former chairman, Sir Angus Watson (both were Congregationalists). The hope was that a Nixon nephew would take over but this plan collapsed when he decided to become a missionary. As there was no other suitable candidate, Isaac Nixon approached Sir Angus and the members rubber-stamped the deal. Of the forty-two members of the Crown who bothered to attend the meeting to approve the transfer of engagements only three voted against. The following year, the Northern Counties took over the Elswick Building Society after a phone call to Market Street one Saturday morning. The message was: 'Please come and see us – we want you to take us over.' And that, despite an earlier Elswick flirtation with the Rock, was that. But the big prize, the Rock itself, remained tantalisingly just out of reach.

Gridlock at the junction of Westgate Road and Collingwood Street, 1950s.

The two societies may have been similar in many respects but they had very different cultures, stemming largely from the character of their respective boards. The Rock men were the Cavaliers, a cross-section of the local aristocracy, their friends and their associates. The Northern Counties people were the Roundheads: tradesmen, chartered accountants, surveyors, estate agents, solicitors and the like. One man who joined Northern Counties as an 18-year-old two years before the merger describes the Market Street office as 'a very tightly-run, very efficient shop. The atmosphere was not unpleasant in any way, but everybody knew their place, and nobody was left in any doubt that you were there to work and get on with it.' The Rock, by contrast, was thought to be a little more happy-go-lucky.

Officially the reasons why the talks led nowhere for eight years was because of a failure to agree over what were described as 'administrative matters'. This was a euphemism. Ridley was every bit as much a hands-on chairman as Osborn was a hands-on executive and everybody realised it could be difficult for the two men to work smoothly together.

The problem was resolved in February 1964 when Ridley died suddenly after an operation to amputate his left leg. In the annual report for that year, the new chairman, Roy Dickinson, in paying tribute to Lord Ridley, reminded members just what a polymath he had been. 'In retrospect, it is difficult to credit that his successful chairmanship of your Society formed only a small part of his business life which embraced the University, the County Council, the Territorial Army, Banking, Insurance and much of the industrial activity of the North of England.'

But by the time the report appeared in the summer of 1964, the union was virtually complete. The ice had been broken by a summit meeting barely four months after Ridley's death. Dickinson was there for the Rock while the Northern Counties sent its chairman, Mould-Graham, and, signif-

A Rock advertisement, not long before the merger.

BUYING A HOUSE ?

WE INVITE YOU TO
CALL IN FOR A CHAT

A speedy and efficient
Mortgage Service

'Generous Advances
and easy
Repayment terms

ROCK
BUILDING
SOCIETY

Head Office :
MARKET STREET,
NEWCASTLE UPON TYNE
Telephone : 28956

Assets exceed £16,000,000 Reserves £668,000

Roy Dickinson succeeded Lord
Ridley as chairman of the Rock in
1964, and was chairman of
Northern Rock from 1967 to 1972.

icantly Osborn himself. Once it had been established that Osborn would be in day-to-day charge of the merged society, other matters like pensions, salaries and so forth were quickly resolved. On 8 June the Rock directors learned the details. As the two societies were of very similar size and weight (Northern Counties had 7,024 members while the Rock had 6,856), it seemed logical that each society should provide an equal number of directors – six or seven apiece. It was agreed that the Northern Counties' Mould-Graham should be chairman for the first two years, and that the deputy chairman should be a Rock man. The Rock board was told that: 'Osborn had been managing director for five years, and there was a strong feeling amongst Northern Counties directors that he should retain that position with the merged Society.' To balance things, the Rock's general manager, the agreeable George Robson would do the same job with the new society; similarly Alan Gilchrist, currently deputy general manger of Rock, would become assistant general manager of the enlarged society, while Ray Chapman, the Rock's man in London, would be assistant general manager (London).

On 8 July, the news was broken to the world.

The amalgamation, [the official press release said] will avoid further duplication of Branch and Head Office services, hasten the introduction of techniques which are in the interests of both members and staffs and establish an extensive Branch and Agency system covering most of the United Kingdom. Furthermore, the housing and savings services of the more broadly based organisation will be able to play a fuller part in the expanding economy of the country. The combined Total Assets of the Societies at 31st December 1964 are expected to be approximately £60 million.

It would have been much simpler, and much less expensive, if the Rock had agreed to a transfer of engagements – a take-over in building society language. But this was vetoed by Rock directors on the grounds that it would have sent a plain signal that the Rock was the weaker party.

The union of the Rock and the Northern Counties meant that the merged society was by far the largest and strongest building society in the north-east with about two-thirds of the region's mortgage business and investment business. With assets that had climbed to £66 million by the year-end, Northern Rock was five times larger than the two next-largest Newcastle-based societies, the Grainger and Percy and the Newcastle Permanent which had fallen badly behind since its heyday in the 1930s. Nonetheless, compared to the giants of the industry, such as the Halifax, the Abbey National, the Co-operative Permanent and Woolwich Equitable, Northern Rock was still a comparative minnow. In the BSA's list of top building societies for 1965, the Northern Rock is ranked at number 16, just behind the Hastings and Thanet and the Cheltenham and Gloucester. With assets of

Facing page: Leeds branch office

£927 million, the Halifax was fourteen times bigger than its newborn northern neighbour. For all its ambitions, Northern Rock was still very much a creature of its native city. Its Market Street offices took 30 per cent of all new investment and were responsible of 20 per cent of mortgage assets, so the board was told. Market Street was special. The board agreed that people should not be allowed to form the opinion that 'we had abandoned the City of our origin or had relegated it in our minds to the status of an ordinary branch.'

With the creation of Northern Rock, Osborn's expansion plans really took off. Broadly speaking, the strategy consisted of three main elements: mergers and acquisitions; the drive for cash; and new technology in the shape of computers and accounting machines. Northern Rock was, of course, not the only building society with these priorities. The number of building societies had been falling continuously from an estimated peak of 3,500 in 1890 as the smaller societies either went out of business or were swallowed up by the larger ones. By 1953 the number of surviving societies had fallen to 782; by 1978, 25 years later, thanks largely to mergers and takeovers, the total had more than halved to 316. But as the number of

THE TIMES

WEDNESDAY JULY 8 1964

BUILDING SOCIETIES IN £60M. MERGER

FROM OUR CITY EDITOR

The Northern-Counties Permanent and the Rock building societies, both with head offices in Newcastle upon Tyne, are to merge their assets into a £60m. society, the Northern Rock Building Society. The merger will place the new society, in terms of assets, among the top flight of societies. There are more than 700 in the country.

It follows one of the biggest building society mergers in recent years between the Bradford Equitable and the Bingley, which became effective from the beginning of this month. The savings in administrative costs and avoidance of further duplication of

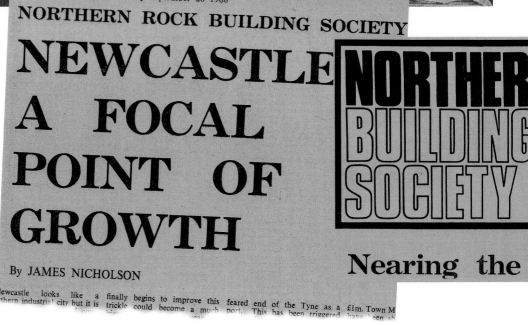

The Northern Counties board, just before the merger.

The Financial Times Thursday September 26 1968

NORTHERN ROCK BUILDING SOCIETY

NEWCASTLE A FOCAL POINT OF GROWTH

By JAMES NICHOLSON

Newcastle looks like a ... rthern industrial city but it is ...

finally begins to improve this ... trickle could become a much ...

feared end of the Tyne as a ... port. This has been triggered ...

£1m. Town M... ... ee sh...

NORTHER BUILDING SOCIETY

Nearing the

societies fell, the number of branches increased as the larger societies extended their reach to all parts of the country. During the 10 years from 1968 to 1978, the number of branches more than doubled from 1,662 to 4,411. The rush for branches became so intense that it led to a town like Bournemouth with a population of 150,000 having twenty-three building society offices, fifteen of them in a single street. Osborn's Northern Rock was also gripped by branch fever. But the important thing was that the union with the Rock gave Osborn, for the first time, the opportunity and the resources to put all three parts of his grand plan into effect. From 1966 onwards, there was action on all fronts.

One of the first societies to succumb to Northern Rock's new urge for acquisition was the Workington Permanent Building Society which Osborn and Rule had been pursuing for at least three years. Shortly after his arrival in Newcastle, Osborn had met Philip Monkhouse, the manager of the Northern Counties' Carlisle branch, and a member of a prominent Cumbrian family. And though Osborn was the boss and Monkhouse the subordinate, Osborn came to admire Monkhouse for both his personal and business qualities.

Computer will handle 150,000 accounts

By TED SCHOETERS

...type are being opened each   operates is a fast 1,350 lines per   The system specified for the   been
...printer which, apart from   company will have both magne-   mach
                                                              magnetic disc   As

RO

gical £100m.

Facing page and above left: The wisdom of the merger would soon be abundantly clear. Press comment was typified by this *Financial Times* report, September 1968.

Left: Foyer of the new offices from the same report: ' The new offices of the Northern Rock may be considered emblematic of the inherent strength of the group.'

In the 1960s colour appeared in people's homes and lives as never before.

The Six-Day Arab-Israeli War, 1967, hastened the downturn in an already ailing economy.

It was Monkhouse who led Osborn to Workington. 'It was one of our most important leaps,' says Osborn. 'We tried and tried and eventually got it on the third time of asking.' Osborn remembers going to a members' meeting and talking to a man in a cloth cap who ran an ice-cream parlour who had been critical of the deal. But when Osborn asked him if he was going to oppose it this time he replied 'I suppose not'. Osborn took this as a signal that success was at hand.

By the early 1970s, the takeover boom was well under way. Between 1971 and 1981 Northern Rock took over twenty-two societies. Most of them were in the north-east and the north-west but as the 1970s were coming to an end, Osborn looked further afield – northwards to Scotland where the Falkirk was acquired in 1978 and as far south as Deal and Walmer which was taken over the following year. Deal was an anomaly: it was so far from the home base that staff joked that it was closer to Germany than Newcastle, but most of the acquisitions fitted in much more neatly and nearly all of them succumbed without a struggle. Even if Osborn had wanted to use a big stick, it would rarely have been needed. The smaller societies were ripe for plucking and often a simple letter of invitation would do the trick. In other cases, Northern Rock resorted to incentives in the shape of bonuses for investors and seats on the local boards for the directors. Such sweeteners were, it found, usually more than enough to persuade societies to fold their tents and join the Northern Rock camp.

By 1967, as Rob Mould-Graham stepped down to be replaced as chairman by Roy Dickinson, the branch network was spreading beyond the north-east with new offices in Birmingham and Nottingham. Already management's eyes were on the new towns of Newton Aycliffe, Peterlee, and Washington New Town in the north-east and Stevenage in the south. London too was a target. The previous year Osborn had picked on a young man called Leo Finn who had made his mark as a sales rep for the north-east. When summoned, Finn thought he was going to Birmingham and was horrified to learn that it was to be Croydon. 'I had never heard of Croydon,' said Finn. By sending one of his own northern managers to London, Osborn was, so Finn believes, trying to counteract the prevailing Rock culture in the south. 'One of the ways of doing this,' Finn says, 'was to infiltrate some people into the south perhaps . . . to undermine this southern power base and demonstrate that his men could do better than the southern managers.' But this was not the only reason why Osborn sent Finn to London.

In the years before and immediately after the Second World War the main preoccupation of building societies had been to attract as much mortgage business as they could. But now with the end of cheap money and stable interest rates, the emphasis shifted. As Fuller Osborn himself remarked in an essay on building society history written 20 years later: 'In the 1960s building societies were learning, perhaps for the first time, that their problem would be to attract sufficient retail money to fund the demand for mortgages.'

By 1966, the economy under Labour was in trouble. The prices and incomes freeze of that year was followed in 1967 by a balance of payments crisis, the devaluation of the pound, and a jump in Bank Rate to 8 per cent. On top of this was the closure of the Suez Canal, and the Six-Day War between Egypt and Israel. By the spring of 1969, building societies were paying savers 5 per cent on their shares and the cost of mortgages had risen to 8.5 per cent – less than the yield on gilts. Even at this level, demand for mortgages remained very high and building societies had to fight fiercely for retail savings.

It was in London and the south-east, that the demand for mortgages was strongest. And the problem was that the Rock's London offices were not earning their keep. They sold plenty of mortgages, but they were not pulling in enough investment money to fund them. Finn's mission was to help in a modest way to reverse this trend. He did not make a promising start. As he recalls:

The Falkirk Building Society was one of Northern Rock's acquisitions in the 1970s.

> In the first 13 months, I took in less money every month than my predecessor. I felt absolutely hopeless. Then suddenly things turned up and we had record takings for the next four years. The biggest asset of a branch manager was energy. And it was used making deals with estate agents and solicitors. They had the clients, you, the building society, had that very precious thing, the loan. So we did trade-offs. We made loans to their clients and they persuaded their clients to lend money to us. One of the reasons I did so well was that I ran the local rugby team which consisted of lawyers, accountants and estate agents. And the price they paid was the money they invested in Northern Rock. There were these little circles passing business around to each other. Typical club, really.

Anxious as it was for more investment business, the society, as ever, remained cautious. In March 1967 the board unanimously followed Osborn's lead and rejected the suggestion that they should issue new-fangled term shares. 'The present time was not opportune for Northern Rock to depart so radically from their well-established practices,' Osborn opined. 'Few societies of substance were currently issuing shares of their nature.' Osborn may have been conservative in fiscal matters but he was also a pragmatist. Four years later, the board decided that in the light of changing circumstances the society 'should be able to launch a new share of this nature without delay'. Shortly afterwards Northern Rock issued its first term shares: ten years later they had become so popular that of the

Housing Minister Richard
Crossman introduced a subsidy
scheme to help with mortgage
payments in 1965.

£14.4 million share and deposit surplus, term shares were on a par with preference and paid-up shares.

Another example of Osborn's readiness to swim with the tide, was the society's belated decision to support the government's option mortgage scheme. Concerned that the poorer sections of the community earned too little to benefit from mortgage tax relief, the Housing Minister, Richard Crossman, introduced a scheme to give people an option of a direct subsidy on their mortgage payments instead of tax relief. Initially the building societies had given the plan such a rough reception that Crossman was obliged to take steps to try and smooth things over. From his diaries it's clear that Crossman found it hard to strike the right note even though he approved of the principle of owner-occupation. 'I had to deliver the speech . . . to the somnolent members of some twenty-six building societies,' he wrote. 'They couldn't have been less interested but they provided me with an occasion for enunciating a philosophy in favour of owner-occupation.' Even so, it seems to have taken some time to bring Northern Rock round as it was not until July 1967, nearly 18 months later, that it voiced its approval – and even then its support was heavily qualified. The board agreed to back the scheme for new and existing borrowers but only on condition that those deciding to stay put were not discriminated against.

It was, perhaps, an unpromising time for Northern Rock to be opening its first-ever custom-built headquarters. But from the moment the merger had been mooted, it was obvious that the offices in Market Street would not do. Even though the Northern Counties was planning to extend round the corner into Pilgrim Street, the existing offices in Market Street were simply too small to house the headquarters staff of the new organisation. It was felt that the best plan was to go for a custom-built office on a greenfield site where there would be room for car parking and future expansion. A number of options were considered. Among them was the old Cochran-Carr brickworks at Cowgate, the former CWS factory at Benton Road, a development in the city centre near the Pilgrim Street roundabout and 1½ acres of council-owned land at the Regent Farm estate, right on the edge of the city at Gosforth. It took the committee, set up to look into the question of new office and chaired by the society's vice chairman, Viscount Ridley, son of the former Rock chairman, nearly a year, but on 21 June 1965 it finally came down in favour of Gosforth and offered the owners, Gosforth Urban District Council, £32,500 for the freehold. The project was given the go-ahead ten days later when, on 1 July 1965, the board of Northern Rock met for the first time.

Designed by Richard Turley & Associates, the nine-storey office block, with its fine views to the Cheviots, looked somewhat out of place on the edge of suburban Gosforth. But as one of the tallest buildings outside the city centre it sent out a strong message – Northern Rock has arrived! It was one of the first offices to be fully air-conditioned and the facilities, which included a modern canteen, were first class. There was plenty of parking space and room at the back for expansion. In fact the building was bigger than was at first needed and initially the top three floors were leased out to ICI.

The building of the Gosforth office was not without its problems. When the contractors' estimates came in, even the lowest, from Sir Robert McAlpine at £705,948, was £30–40,000 higher than expected. But after some helpful suggestions from the architect and quantity surveyor, which cut £20,000 from the price, what was hoped would be a final figure of £685,006 15s. was agreed and work began.

Another early shot of the headquarters at Gosforth.

Main Edinburgh branch.

8

Branch Fever

By the winter of 1967-68, the new head office building was ready for topping out and the Duke of Northumberland had agreed to perform the opening ceremony which had been set for Thursday, 26 September 1968. There was to be a champagne buffet lunch for 200 special guests and a cocktail party for staff and their partners a week later. It was decided that as a thank-you present the Duke should be given a colour TV. Over the next ten days, Northern Rock was to hold open house to allow all its friends and professional contacts to come and admire the brand new office. But there was more to the building than making room for all the extra bodies.

For some time before the move to Gosforth, it was clear that Northern Rock would have to computerise. As it would take the society into strange and unknown territory, the big decisions were left until after the building project was more or less out of the way. The first task was to choose the hardware. There were three possible manufacturers: NCR, IBM and ICL. The board would have liked to stay with NCR as the society was already using its cash machines but the firm's current computer was on the way out and the new model would not be ready in time. That left the Americans in the shape of IBM and the British ICT, then in the process of becoming the Government-backed ICL.

First on the list was ICL. As ICL had no representative in the north-east, a party from Northern Rock travelled down to Bracknell in Berkshire where the firm had its HQ. The visitors were under the impression that they were ICL's guests so they were somewhat put out when the managing director, whom they thought was the host, handed them the bill for the evening dinner at the hotel. They were scarcely mollified when he invited them back to his house for coffee. The visit to IBM, by contrast, could not have gone better. The Americans, who made their pitch at the head office of the Leeds

At Northern Rock House for the opening ceremony, left to right, Fuller Osborn, chief executive, the Duke of Northumberland, and Roy Dickinson, chairman.

Above and facing page: an ICL computer of the same generation as the ICT 1902A, ordered by Northern Rock in 1968.

Permanent, put on a very polished performance. The Leicester Permanent who were the first to computerise also had their brains picked.

Rather than take the plunge on its own, the team, who privately favoured IBM, sought the advice of a firm of consultants called Mouncey and Partners who had designed a £34,000 computer package for building societies. Their clients included the Temperance, the Alliance and the Northampton Town and Country. Northern Rock was somewhat dismayed when Mouncey recommended ICL but felt it had no option but to accept the experts' choice. As the computer had to be up and running well before D-Day in February 1971 when Britain switched to decimal currency, there was no time for delay. Accordingly on 20 March 1968 the board agreed to purchase an ICT 1902A computer.

The contract was signed a week later on 27 May 1968. With all its disc drives, printers and other bits and pieces, the cost of the 64K machine with a 16MB hard disc was around £150,000. A dozen years later, home computers with the same specification were selling in high street stores for a few hundred pounds. It was, nonetheless, no toy. It took a great deal of effort and money to install: Mouncey's bill doubled to £60,000 and the firm went bankrupt before the job was finished. But the computer handled all the cash, investment and mortgage business easily enough. And when decimalisation came, the conversion was done in under three hours.

In December 1969, just over 18 months after the order had been placed, Alan Gilchrist, the deputy general manager, reported that the computer had taken over and balanced the subscription account. For the first time, he said, it was true to say that the computer was making a positive contribution

to the organisation. Two years later, the computer was processing all 50,000 borrowers' accounts as well as the 160,000 investment accounts.

1969 was a watershed year for the Northern Rock and for its chief executive, Fuller Osborn. In that year Northern Rock's assets passed the £100 million mark and Osborn was elected chairman of the Building Societies Association. For a society which was still firmly in the second division (it ranked only sixteenth or seventeenth in size) this was a signal honour. It was a recognition that Northern Rock was a force to be reckoned with. It was also a reward to Osborn himself, who had been a member of the council of the BSA since 1956, for long and faithful service to the movement.

'Fuller was a fully paid-up member of the chief executive's club of the BSA,' says Leo Finn, the present chief executive of Northern Rock. 'He always played by the rules. He always opposed anything that would cause him difficulty as regional chairman or later as a council member or chairman.' Physically, he was an upright, imposing figure with a sharp, hawk-like profile and a penetrating eye. He tended to judge people by their sporting prowess – especially cricket. He also had a very soft spot for his fellow Gunners or anyone who, like himself, had had a good war. His relations with his subordinates were cordial enough, though he did have his favourites. On his regular tours of the branches, he always took the manager out to lunch as part of the ritual. But all the same they were always on their best behaviour. 'He commanded respect,' says one former branch manager. 'He only had to look at you and you'd just wither.'

It is perhaps fortunate that Osborn took over at the BSA at a quiet time, after the more turbulent George Brown/Richard Crossman years. As he

The order form for Northern Rock's first computer. Note the price – today's equivalent of about £1.2 million – and the memory of the processor: 16K!

Above: Northern Rock offices,
2 Market Street, 1971, and
(*below*) today.

himself says: 'Everything went very smoothly. The chairman could speak for the movement with confidence, knowing he would be supported. It was also a time of interest rate stability. During those two years, from April 1969 to November 1971, the council made no recommendation to change either the mortgage rate, then 8½ per cent, or the ordinary share rate, then 5 per cent. And, of course, we were not offering, as we are now, a multitude of other rates to savers.' Osborn plainly enjoyed the ceremonial and social side of the work, with its frequent trips to distant places, talking home loans and making new friends in New Zealand or South Africa. What made it even more pleasant was the established convention that wives went too at the society's expense.

It was not just the BSA that made up Osborn's public life. He also became, as Lord Ridley had been before him, a major figure in the affairs of the north-east. He started in 1967 as a member of the board of the Washington Development Corporation. Two years later, in the same year as he became chairman of the BSA, he joined the North-East Planning Council, where he was later to become number two to the chairman, Councillor T. Dan Smith, who was to fall from grace as a result of the Poulson affair. The work for the BSA and the North-East Planning Council brought Osborn close to

government while his chairmanship of Newcastle's Union Club meant that he was on Christian name terms with most of the north-east's movers and shakers. Osborn was a man who wanted to exercise his power and found a provincial area in which he could exercise it across a very wide range.

Even though these public activities took up a great deal of Osborn's energy and time, he was still thinking about how to develop the business. In July 1970, the forthcoming retirement of George Robson as general manager and secretary after 46 years' service, gave Osborn the opportunity to reorganise the business on more modern lines and to promote his most trusted lieutenants. Robson, who had stepped up to be general manager of the Rock in 1956 after the unexpected retirement of his predecessor, Ralph Cotton, was by general agreement an excellent second-in-command and a very nice man. But it was now time for a new and, on the whole, better educated generation to take over. As from 31 December 1970, the top tier would consist of Osborn himself with the title of chief executive, his deputy Alan Gilchrist, and assistant general manager, E. J. Morrison. What was new, however, was the creation of a team of five 'controllers' with specific line responsibilities. Fifty-four-year-old Philip Monkhouse took charge of development, John English, 39, became the finance man, 55-year-old Arthur Rule was given management services, Matthew Atthey, 62, was the mortgage controller and Douglas Urwin, 45, looked after the staff. The idea was to push responsibility for the day-to-day administration down the line, while giving the line managers more say in policy-making by membership of a newly created 'chief officers committee'.

It was no longer possible to run something as large as Northern Rock on the personal, paternalistic lines of the old Northern Counties with its strict timekeeping and its even stricter hierarchies. The 1970s was a period when the trade unions were exercising their power and even as unmilitant a body as the largely female, white-collar workforce of Northern Rock was not immune to the trade union rhetoric of the time. This period saw the formation of an embryonic trade union in the shape of a staff association which, although it lacked wage negotiating rights, was heavily involved in grading and job evaluation. It also had a say about working conditions and other practical matters.

The first leader of the staff association was, oddly enough, the same Leo Finn who had been handpicked by Osborn to go to London and who 20 years later was to become chief executive. At that time, Finn had the reputation of being, by building society standards, something of a left-winger – a trait he inherited from his father who had worked as a day labourer on a farm and then as charge-hand in a pumping station. Finn père was a socialist of the old school. His son campaigned for Shelter and came to work on a bicycle which he parked in the banking hall. 'I had a wonderful plot to make the thing a worker's co-operative with profit sharing but it was all thrown out and we ended up with a bog standard agreement between employer and employee,' he recalls. Northern Rock's

T. Dan Smith, whose powerful chairmanship of the North-East Planning Council in the 1960s came to an end as a result of his business involvement with John Poulson (*below*).

Harold Wilson (right), Prime Minister, with Alderman Andy Cunningham who was later discredited by the Poulson affair.

The Conservatives came to power, with Edward Heath as Prime Minister, in 1970.

Facing page: Manchester branch.

Joint meeting of the main board and the London board of Northern Rock, late 1970s.

attitude to staff relations was neither reactionary nor progressive. 'There was never a desire to go against what was happening in society,' Finn says. 'But it would never take the lead. Once it had made up its mind, it did the job properly.' In 1971, Finn was put in charge of staff training.

The following year the society took a step that was to have a profound effect on its future. In launching its graduate trainee scheme, Northern Rock broke with a tradition going back more than a century. Instead of hiring young clerks straight from school, Northern Rock started to trawl the universities for talent. The early 1970s saw the recruitment of an entirely new generation of graduate managers whose talents came into full play in the late 1980s and early 1990s. Only two, Keith Currie and Kevin Southwood, had any business expertise: the others were lawyers, linguists, sociologists, and economists.

The period of Osborn's chairmanship of the BSA was one in which the price of new houses rose sharply. It was the beginning of the luckless Barber boom. By the end of 1970 the price of new houses had increased by 6.5 per cent. Even so, demand for mortgages continued to accelerate as people realised that inflation was making their mortgages look cheap. Building societies entered a period of rapid growth: instead of 12 to 15 per cent, they started expanding by 20 per cent or more. In just four years, between 1969 and 1973, the Northern Rock's assets doubled from £100m. to £200 million.

By 1973, in the wake of the Yom Kippur War and the subsequent oil crisis, the economic waters had become distinctly choppy. The first half of the year saw the BSA-recommended rate to investors rise three times in five months as societies sought to stem a haemorrhaging of funds. The Northern Rock was so worried that in April of that year it sold £2.7 million-worth of gilts to bolster £7.8 million of current funds. The managing director reported that unless interest rates stabilised, or preferably fell, it was likely that the

heavy drain on the society's funds would continue for some time. However, he was soon proved wrong. After the year's third rise in May, lifting the investors' rate to 6.75 per cent, the society took in £7.3 million – an all-time record for a single month.

It was at this point that Matthew Atthey, the mortgage controller, decided to call it a day after 48 years with the society. Atthey was one of the old school who joined Northern Counties five years before Arthur Rule. In his farewell speech, he reminded his listeners that he had served under eight of the society's ten chairmen and for three out of the four chief executives. His was a voice from a past that now seemed incredibly far away. In those days rates remained unchanged for decades: now, it seemed, hardly a month went by without another upset.

Barely had Atthey walked out of the door, when the interest-rate roundabout started up again. In July, the Northern Rock followed the BSA's lead in announcing a 0.35 per cent reduction in rates as from 1 September. However, the inflow of new money fell so dramatically that half-way through August, the movement changed its mind, rescinded the July announcement, and ruled that rates would remain unchanged. A month later, it announced a 0.75 per cent increase for investors and a hefty 1 per cent rise for borrowers.

The ups and downs of 1973 made everybody, including the financial controller, very nervous of forecasting the outcome of 1974. As he told the board: 'Though an estimated monthly investment surplus of £1.5 million at present seemed high, in more normal times, with assets of £216 million, the Society would have expected this figure to be in the region of £2.5 million a month.' But the emphasis on surplus or net funding was changing. The volatility of the mortgage market caused the Northern Rock, like other building societies, to look much more closely at its margins and to pay less attention to those traditional measures, volume and asset growth. As Leo Finn says:

> Suddenly profitability became more important than volume business. We had never measured profit before. We hadn't looked at where the profits came from. We didn't understand what was driving the profit. The society had so much old business on its books that the problem was how to allocate the profit from that. What we didn't realise was that we weren't making any profit from the new business going forward. It was being subsidised by the old business on the books. And so we started to make models of branch profitability.

The mid-1970s was a time when branch fever was at its height. But though Northern Rock's takeover techniques were by now finely honed, there were failures. One that caused the most heartache was the aborted merger with the Eastbourne Mutual which was called off in February 1974. As Arthur Rule tells the story:

The miners' industrial action in 1974 led to a national three-day week and the fall of the Heath government.

A friendship had built up between Gilbert Anderson, the general manager of the Eastbourne who later became its chairman, and Fuller Osborn when he had been deputy chairman of the BSA during Anderson's term as chairman. Discussions subsequently took place and progressed almost to special general meeting stage. Unfortunately Anderson's successor as general manager was not in favour of the merger and he mustered support from the professional men in Eastbourne and their campaign reached front page headlines in the local press as a result of which the Directors got cold feet and called it off . . . We later learned that particularly the branch staff were most disappointed as they felt it would have been in their best interests and the members were quite annoyed as they had been done out of a one per cent bonus.

The Eastbourne affair took place at a time of national crisis. The miners' challenge to the Heath government led directly to the three-day week, followed by the calling of a general election at which Heath was defeated by Harold Wilson. Housing was high on the new government's agenda. In

Durham Miners' Gala parade, 1974. Banners indicate the range of support for the miners in their dispute.

an attempt to stimulate a flagging building programme where private-sector building was at its lowest for 15 years, Harold Wilson offered the building societies a loan of £500 million at a fixed rate of 10.5 per cent. Of this sum, Northern Rock received just over £8 million. This injection, plus a sudden inflow of term share money, meant that the society was able to reverse its policy, set earlier in the year, of cutting back its mortgage commitments to a minimum.

The failure at Eastbourne had been offset by a whole string of successes elsewhere. In December of 1974 came the first incursion into Scotland with the takeover of the Edinburgh-based Prudential Investment Building Society. In Osborn's absence in London the deal was done, between Arthur Rule and Bill Moodie, the Prudential's chairman, in a local golf club over a couple of double gins. The following year, Northern Rock strengthened its local base still further with the acquisitions of the building societies at Haltwhistle and Wallsend. Over the next four years, from 1975 to 1979, mergers came thick and fast; in all there were fourteen. And in 1978, the Northern Rock greatly strengthened its base in Scotland with the acquisition of the Falkirk.

In that same year, David Martin who had joined the Northern Counties as an 18-year-old clerk two years before the merger, got his first post as a branch manager when he was sent to South Shields. He had worked his way up the ladder as a back office man – first as assistant cashier, then chief cashier, and then assistant manager – until he was the most senior person in the office never to have worked in a branch. At that time, the branch was

David Martin: his first post as branch manager was at South Shields.

South Shields viewed from Tynemouth.

Kenneth Clark (left) had taken over as chairman from Rendell Bartlett in 1976.

Jimmy Carter, the US President, on a visit to Newcastle. Jim Callaghan, the Prime Minister, is second from the right, and Fuller Osborn is fifth from the left.

the pivot around which the building society movement revolved. 'The branch manager's job was the one that everybody aimed at,' he said. 'You had staff, a recognised position in local society and a car.' Interviewed 20 years later, he still remembers the car. 'It was a Talbot Horizon – the first new car I had ever owned.'

It wasn't until I got there that I realised what a close-knit community it was: solicitors, bank managers, estate agents. It wasn't a question of selling Northern Rock. It was a question of selling oneself. The priority was to raise investment money. As the local solicitors and accountants often acted as financial advisers to their clients they were in a position to give us a lot of business. But they were giving money to you as opposed to the organisation. So you had to get to know everybody. Social events like the Building Societies Institute annual dinner were very important. It was held at the Seaburn Hotel in Sunderland. Everybody who was anybody wanted to get to the BSI dinner. Likewise it was equally important for me to be seen at their professional association dinners. I was nervous about not being invited in case my bosses (who were) would notice my absence and think I was falling down on the job. So I used to wave at everybody, just so they would remember me.

By the time Dave Martin had got his job at South Shields, the Osborn era was coming to a close. He had seen Northern Rock grow from a middle-ranking society with assets of £66 million to one with over £500 million. The society's position in the league table had changed very little and one or two regional societies, notably the Bristol and West and, to a lesser degree, the Cheltenham and Gloucester, had outpaced the northern society. But that is hardly surprising. Despite its presence in London and forays as far as the south coast of England, Northern Rock remained essentially what its name indicated – a northern building society. A survey of the pattern of lending in 1977, shortly before Osborn retired as chief executive, showed that 60 per cent of its mortgage business was in the four northern counties and 40 per cent was spread around the remainder of the United Kingdom, including Scotland and Northern Ireland. In the face of a widening gap between north and south and the rundown of the north-east's traditional industries, that Northern Rock was able to keep pace with its prosperous southern cousins is a great tribute to Osborn's skill and determination as a manager.

Osborn had not wanted to give up his executive position. But as 1978 came to a close, he was reaching the thirtieth anniversary of his appointment as general manager of Northern Counties and was in his thirteenth year in charge of Northern Rock. At 63 he was, by the standards set by such men as Charles Burney Catnach, comparatively a stripling but his number two, Alan Gilchrist, had been waiting in the wings for far too long and was anxious to show what he could do. It was therefore agreed that Osborn should stand down as chief executive. The chairman's seat was occupied by Kenneth Clark who had taken over two years before from Rendell Bartlett.

Kenneth Clark, chairman, congratulates Arthur Rule on 48 years of service in 1978.

9

The Big Push

Alan Gilchrist, the new chief executive, was unfortunate in two respects. Firstly, he took over from Fuller Osborn at a bad moment. Secondly, he was in poor health. By the beginning of 1979, the Callaghan government had all but lost control of events. The year opened with what the press was to call 'The winter of discontent'. The public sector was in revolt and marked its protest with selective strikes. London was worst affected. The army's 'Green Goddesses' were called out on fire-fighting duty, volunteers were sent in to clear the piles of rubbish from public places like Leicester Square, and schoolchildren went without lunch. The dead were unburied. It was also a time of runaway inflation. House prices, which had risen by a quarter the previous year, were set to increase even further in 1979 and by the summer the cost of an ordinary Northern Rock repayment mortgage had reached 11.75 per cent. By that time, there had been a fundamental change in the political landscape. In May 1979, a demoralised James Callaghan called an election which was won by Margaret Thatcher who had succeeded Heath as leader of the Conservative Party. It took time for the full consequences of the Thatcher victory to become apparent. But the building societies were encouraged that a party with a gut-belief in owner-occupation was once again in charge.

By 1980, the increase in house prices had slowed to 10 per cent compared to a record 29 per cent the previous year. But money remained expensive and interest rates were still very high. While the majority of building societies still remained loyal to the BSA cartel, the smaller and medium-sized societies nibbled at the edges by tempting investors with carefully crafted, high-interest packages. Depending on circumstances, investors could get an annual return of up to 14 per cent gross on their money.

For most of 1980 the attention of the Northern Rock board was on local matters. With the country in the grip of unemployment, 150 steel workers

Glasgow branch.

Alan Gilchrist, chief executive
from 1978 to 1982.

The 'Winter of Discontent'
1978–9: Newcastle city workers
voting to strike.

from West Cumberland wrote to say they were having trouble meeting their mortgage payments. The general manager reported that everything was being done to help them. At the same time, the assistant general manager, in a paper to the board entitled 'Welfare benefits, strikers and the unemployed', noted that the society was having difficulty in recovering mortgage interest payments, as the money was going directly to the individual as part of the supplementary benefit. In addition to these problems, there was the long-running argument with McAlpine's, the builders of the Gosforth head office, over the cost of fixing the leaks that had developed. The eventual bill was £284,000.

By the spring of 1981, however, the board was beginning to worry about the success other societies were having with their new short-term shares, especially the Cheltenham and Gloucester with its instant access 'Cheltenham Gold'. Alan Gilchrist told the board that the lack of such a product was 'affecting our competitive edge, particularly with agents and professional connections' and he suggested that the society should respond, even though it probably would mean 'a considerable transfer from existing accounts'. The board said it would leave it to management to decide whether the new shares were to be an attacking or a defensive measure.

The debate continued. In September, Gilchrist alerted the board to greater competition for investment money and mortgage business on three fronts: National Savings where the government had just launched a new £1,500 million Save-as-you-earn savings drive, the banks who were beginning to go after the mortgage business, and the building societies themselves with their new high-interest products. 'It is almost certain', Gilchrist said, 'that the costs of raising capital will continue to increase.' And he concluded: 'The time is now opportune to consider raising some funds from the Money Market.' The correctness of this analysis was borne out by the November figures which showed that while the ordinary preference share and savings accounts were in deficit, it was the high-yielding term shares that made up the bulk of the £44 million surplus.

For Northern Rock, as for the rest of the building society movement, the early 1980s was a time of agonising reappraisal. The chief executives of the small to medium-sized societies like Northern Rock were in a particular difficulty. Almost wholly dependent on raising money from the small private investor, they lacked the size, the muscle, and, it has to be said, the inclination to go to the City for the extra cash. They were in a Catch-22 situation. If they went hell for leather for expansion, their margins and their reserves would suffer. But if they did nothing, they would be steam-rollered by larger and stronger competitors. In the minutes, the references to other building societies as colleagues and friends began to disappear. Now they were often called predators.

In March 1982, Alan Gilchrist set out for the board his vision of the future. After highlighting the success of the high-interest accounts and dwelling gloomily on the seemingly ever-rising cost of funding, Gilchrist dropped a bombshell. 'The time is probably now opportune', he wrote, 'to consider the wider question of whether we should be giving serious thought to the question of a merger with a society about our own size.' And he concluded that from now on, building societies would find the going much harder. Already banks had taken a quarter of the mortgage market and it was plain they would not stop there. He wrote:

Staff from the Bank Tabungan of Indonesia on a training programme on housing and finance at Northern Rock.

> The change from an industry operating relatively free from external and internal competition to an industry operating in a very competitive environment can be very painful . . . Societies will find it necessary to re-examine their whole method of operation and may well need to look at marketing their mortgage services. The greatest danger is to assume that the relatively easy days of the 1970s will return and that all that needs to be done in the short term is to relax lending criteria or to rely on investing in the gilt market.

The board was so struck by this analysis that it decided to set up a policy committee consisting of the chairman, the deputy chairman, and the

WHAT IS THIS?

An unfamiliar high-tech contraption. Trial model of an ATM, cash dispensing machine, early 1980s.

Fuller Osborn, as first high sheriff
of Tyne and Wear.

managing director to study the subject and report back to the board from
time to time. A month later Fuller Osborn became chairman on the
retirement of Kenneth Clark and by the end of the year, Alan Gilchrist
himself had gone. He had been obliged to retire early on grounds of ill-
health. It was a bitter blow. In the brief time he had been chief executive
not only had he made his mark on the society but, as a member of the
Spalding committee which helped shape the landmark 1986 Building
Societies Act, he had played a part on the national stage.

The man who replaced him was Christopher Sharp, who at the age of 43
was on the threshold of a brilliant career. He took charge at a time when
Northern Rock, like the building society movement as a whole, was growing
at a headlong pace. The economy may have been in poor shape but the
demand for mortgages was unabated. Between 1979 and 1983, helped
greatly by inflation, the society's assets doubled from £500 to £1,000 million.

Like Fuller Osborn, Sharp was not a local man. He was educated at
Stockport Grammar School and Pembroke College, Oxford. After graduating
in 1962, Sharp went into local government as a solicitor for Shropshire
County Council. In 1970 he joined Northern Rock as the society's solicitor
but after a short period left Newcastle to work for the rival Cheltenham and
Gloucester. It was Philip Monkhouse, a close friend of both Sharp and
Osborn, who brokered the reunion by setting up a meeting between
Osborn and the renegade. 'I'll meet you halfway between Gloucester and
Newcastle,' Osborn announced. In the event, the meeting took place just
down the road at the Washington Posthouse!

Sharp moved in to take over the running of Northern Rock's mortgage
department which apparently he did very well. An approachable figure with
a taste for good living, Sharp was the antithesis of the traditional senior
building society executive who tended to be better acquainted with Calvin
than Calvin Klein. Sharp was younger and much more laid-back than
average and, as one of the society's first graduates, he attracted kindred
spirits. He also became, perhaps surprisingly, one of Osborn's protégés.
Those who knew both men well say there was a strong degree of mutual
admiration. Sharp admired what Osborn had done at Northern Rock, and
Osborn saw in Sharp the man he might have been had he had the younger
man's opportunities. When it became clear just how ill Alan Gilchrist was,
there was an in-house competition for the post of deputy chief executive.
Those invited to apply were Ray Chapman, the head of the London office,
John English, the head of finance, John Purdon, the head of development,
and Chris Sharp. Although the smart money was on Purdon and English, it
was Sharp who won.

One of the first things he did on becoming chief executive was to give
the bright young men more scope and more responsibility than they had
previously enjoyed. Many of the class of '72 and their successors began to
come into their own. Those who had joined as callow young graduates
were now seasoned campaigners with ten years experience. Among them

ICL Interchange Centre,
Gateshead, April 1985.

were David Baker, who read sociology (now a main board director), and
Chris Jobe, who obtained his articles in Chris Sharp's legal department
(now group secretary). Other graduate entrants were Kim Barry, now
director of savings, Keith Currie, group treasurer, and Colin Taylor, director
of legal services.

Not every high flyer was a product of the graduate recruitment scheme.
Kevin Southwood came from the world of insurance and made his mark as
the society's first-ever marketing controller. In 1985, he became the first
head of the newly-created business policy unit; rose rapidly to a general
manager's job; and joined the board in 1990. Four years later, he left to join
Alliance & Leicester plc. Adam Applegarth, who joined Northern Rock as a
graduate entrant, followed closely in Southwood's footsteps. After working
in the business policy unit as a research assistant, he took over marketing
in 1990, was appointed a general manager in 1993 and joined the board in
1996 with responsibilities for marketing, loans and IT.

One of the factors behind Northern Rock's outstanding performance in
the years prior to demutualisation was the high quality of its management.
It is notable that four out of the five present-day executive directors have
a university degree and the fifth, Bob Bennett, the finance director, has no
fewer than three accountancy qualifications. After Leo Finn, the longest

One of Northern Rock's more far-flung
agencies: Stornaway, Isle of Lewis.

serving director is David Baker who has worked for Northern Rock for 24 years and is now responsible for a wide portfolio that includes distribution, personnel and training, planning, savings, and commercial lending. By the year 2000, the executive directors had served Northern Rock for a total of 84 years.

On Sharp's arrival some of the older men were pushed aside, sometimes none too gently, to make way for the new technocrats. The young men were given the freedom to have a go at the organisation. London was no longer a separate fiefdom and the power and independence of the branch managers was cut back and brought under central control. The responsibility for marketing passed from the branches to corporate headquarters.

By coincidence, the changes in top management at Northern Rock more or less coincided with the collapse of the BSA's 50-year-old rate-fixing cartel. Sharp had been in his new job no more than eight months when the Abbey National's chairman, Sir Campbell Adamson, gave the BSA three

The first computerisation of the pass book was implemented on a Nixdorf machine in the 1980s. Sylvia Purvis (left) and Fiona Campbell are now senior managers at Northern Rock.

A Northern Rock Homes scheme is opened. Fuller Osborn, right.

month's notice of its intention to leave. This was not the first time the cartel had been under pressure. The Halifax had withdrawn for eight years between 1956 and 1964 and by 1977 the BSA's recommendations were being ignored by one-third of its members. The Abbey National's move proved the final blow. A month later, in September 1983, the BSA's council voted unanimously to end the 50-year-old system. From then on, societies were free to set their own rates of interest.

The collapse of the cartel illustrated just how fiercely the winds of competition were blowing through the financial services business. As Berry Ritchie puts it in his history of the Abbey: 'Abbey National made its decision to leave the cartel for three reasons. Firstly, the rates agreement had served its purpose and was frequently being abused. Secondly, it added to the number and complexity of investment schemes on the market. And thirdly, leaving the cartel allowed the Abbey National to react more quickly to market forces.' As far as Northern Rock was concerned, what was sauce for the goose, was sauce for the gander.

One of the first signs of the new direction at Northern Rock was the setting up of the Northern Rock Housing Trust. At a time of national

Opening a public art project in the Avenues Agency – a housing improvement in Gateshead.

Shields Road Branch, Newcastle.

housing shortage, the building societies were being urged to help local authorities and housing associations to provide for the poorer members of the community who could not afford or did not qualify for conventional mortgages. In December 1983, the Woolwich had announced it had formed a limited company, Woolwich Homes, which would buy land for development to bring home ownership within reach of those who couldn't afford it. The first target was to be the inner cities. The following autumn, the Northern Rock followed suit, the first building society in the north-east to do so.

The move was master-minded by Leo Finn, who strongly believed that societies should play a greater role in direct housing provision, just as the land societies had done more than 130 years before. In a paper to the board, Finn argued that providing houses for sale was no threat to the society's core mortgage business as, in the long run, it would underpin mortgage supply. What he could not guarantee, however, was that the venture would be a financial success and he warned that diversification inevitably involved a degree of risk. In February 1985, the board agreed to go ahead with the first project: the construction of twenty-two flats at Ness Street in Berwick-upon-Tweed. It sanctioned an advance of £700,000 and set an initial rate of interest of 13 per cent plus a share of the profits. The object was a return of 2 per cent above base rate and a £40,000 profit was forecast. However, the board recognised that there might be a loss. Unhappily, the board's fears were justified. In the first 14 months, the company showed a deficit of £78,643, thanks largely to losses on the Berwick scheme.

Faced with increasing competition from the banks and suffering from a legislative straitjacket, the BSA had been pressing for greater commercial freedom for some time. The government responded with the most far-reaching piece of building society legislation for 150 years. The 1986 Building Societies Act answered many of the societies' most immediate needs: amongst other things, it allowed them to raise 20 per cent of their funds from the wholesale markets; to make unsecured personal loans; to own and develop land for housing; to offer pensions and personal equity plans; and to operate in Europe and the Channel Islands. Also, most significantly, it opened the door to conversion from mutual to plc status.

That the Act more or less coincided with a new regime at Northern Rock was fortuitous. But what happened next was not. Sharp and his team moved quickly to take advantage of the new freedoms. In July 1986, within days of the Act receiving Royal assent, the board prepared for the launch of a Northern Rock unit trust by interviewing two firms of investment managers, Martin

Currie Investment Management and Gartmore Investment Management. Four months later, the society, following the lead of the major players, also opened negotiations with two chains of estate agencies.

The business logic behind the move into estate agency seemed to be impeccable. On the face of it, estate agencies seemed ideally placed to cross-sell Northern Rock's mortgages and other related financial products such as insurance. The initial hope was that 'within a year or two', Northern Rock Property Services, as the estate agency business was called, would be the source of a quarter of the society's £400 million a year mortgage business. Even so, the board was cautious. Rather than buying estate agencies outright, the society preferred initially to limit its stake to 50 per cent in each business. Unlike many of its competitors, Northern Rock proceeded on tip toe rather than rushing headlong into the business. Overall it spent some £9 million on buying some 123 outlets in the north-east and the south. The final cost, when accumulated losses are taken into account, was around £20 million. The estate agency venture, which rested on the fallacy that local individual businesses could be institutionalised, turned out to be one of the great business disasters of the decade. The Nationwide lost £200 million building up a chain of over 300 outlets while the Abbey National's Cornerstone operation consumed £258 million. By comparison, Northern Rock escaped quite lightly.

In the spring of 1987 such problems lay in the future. With total assets now in excess of £1,800 million, record profits of £15 million, a record inflow of funds from investors and a growth rate of over 15 per cent, Northern Rock seemed to be in fine shape. In his last speech as chairman, Fuller Osborn tried to strike a positive note. There were, he said, particular opportunities in the pension market arising from reforms in social security legislation; there had been a successful pilot of an unsecured lending package; the housing trust was making headway; and the society was about to take a stake in the estate agency business.

But the tone was not uniformly upbeat. Reporting on the housing market, Osborn told members that there were wide gaps between the south of England where house price inflation reached 24 per cent in parts of London and the north where prices rose by 5 per cent on average. 'The north-south debate', he said, 'will no doubt continue . . . I need only say that house price disparities of such proportions make no sense in overall economic or social terms.' In view of what was to come, his next remarks were prescient. 'A feature of the year has been media comment on excessive borrowing by individuals and families. We at Northern Rock have always been particularly careful to advise our borrowers not to take on too great a repayment commitment. Yet

The 'Big Bang' in the Stock Exchange, and deregulation, combined with the property boom of the mid-1980s symbolised by Canary Wharf, were soon to be followed by recession at the end of the decade.

the level of arrears among the Society's borrowers continues to rise . . . We provide counselling services but we cannot help in every case. We cannot mend broken marriages nor can we mitigate the effects of long-term unemployment.' Within nine months, Northern Rock's assets had passed the £2,000 million mark, causing the *Financial Times* to comment: 'Steady progress for Northern Rock.'

As London house inflation roared upwards over the next 18 months, the Newcastle team decided not to join the party. 'We were very struck by the silly things that were going on – developers giving away Porsches to buyers of houses in Docklands and that sort of thing,' Leo Finn recalls. 'It seemed to us fundamentally stupid. At the same time we were having difficulty raising funds. So it meant we took a very low-risk attitude to lending.' But as boom turned into slump, the society was to find that its prudence had paid off handsomely.

Of course Northern Rock did not escape the effects of the recession entirely. The sustained level of interest rates resulted in a significant increase in the number of borrowers unable to meet their monthly payments. And rising unemployment swelled the numbers still further.

By the autumn of 1990, the number of borrowers who were more than six months in arrears had risen from 1,200 in 1989 to 2,800. Even so, with only 159 properties in possession, and with only 0.004 per cent of its mortgage advances in arrears, the society was vastly better off than most of its competitors. As Finn explains:

When the bubble burst it meant that because we hadn't taken much money and we hadn't lent much in London,

A Northern Rock Homes development, (*above*), in Tynemouth, viewed (*main picture*) from the north looking towards South Shields.

The Prince of Wales is presented with a donation to the Princes Trust by Lord Ridley. Chris Sharp is second from the left.

our provisions were very low. Not only were we getting a cost advantage over our competitors but we had a provision advantage which was huge. Our rivals had to close their doors and stop lending to protect their balance sheets. Everybody was frightened by what had happened. But we realised that the market was fundamentally sound. There is no substitute for owner-occupation. And provided we had the right people with the right credit history, it was time to open up and grow. There was no competition. We could make good margins, while growing at a rapid rate.'

1991 was a remarkably good year for Northern Rock, with asset growth of 29 per cent and an outstanding 31 per cent increase in net profits. Where previously its regional character had been a definite handicap, now it proved a positive advantage. As Chris Sharp, who had followed in Fuller Osborn's footsteps as chairman of the BSA in 1991, remarked pithily: '1991 has probably seen the worst recession in the housing market since the Second World War . . . Northern Rock avoided the worst of it because it was in the north and the slump was in the south.' As Sharp saw it, the challenge was to find a way of building on the advantage. Outlining the prospects for 1992, he wrote: 'We must change our temporary advantage arising from others' distress over mortgage losses into a lasting cost advantage and we must do this before other societies start unwinding their provision levels.' In conclusion he posed three questions: Can we maintain our increased market share whilst achieving our profit targets? Can we continue our rapid growth whilst containing our increase in costs? Can we get our cost ratios at least into the 'pack' before our competitors sort out their mortgage loans and come 'hot foot' after us?

Costs were indeed a problem. A study of building society performance by the brokers, UBS Phillips & Drew, only a few months earlier illustrated the extent to which Northern Rock had stolen a march on the pack. Of the top thirteen societies, the brokers reported, only three had grown faster than Northern Rock; the society was fifth overall in terms of asset growth and fifth in terms of profit:earnings ratio. But the study also revealed that Northern Rock was not as tightly managed as it should have been. Measured by management expenses as a percentage of total income, Northern Rock ranked only seventeenth in the league table.

The brokers' findings came as no surprise. The society had been struggling to reduce its management expenses for the last couple of years but with only limited success. 'Years of a relatively easy life had not been conducive to the creation of a cost-aware culture in the society,' Leo Finn told the board in the autumn of 1991. 'The budgetary process had too much emphasis on central control and managers were easily able to avoid personal responsibility for their own costs; this being particularly true of staff costs.' It was only after the decision had been taken to kill off the loss-making estate agency venture, which was sold in the course of 1992, that some real headway was made.

Of equal, if not greater importance, was the launch of the postal account in February 1992. Up until that point, all the growth in net retail deposits had been generated solely by the branches, the majority of which were in the north. The object of the postal account was to attract money from outside the traditional areas covered by the branches. This proved so successful that within six months over 84 per cent of all new money was coming from outside the traditional northern region.

For all the emphasis on increased managerial and operating efficiency, mergers and acquisitions remained the key element in Sharp's strategy for long-term survival. As Northern Rock's reputation for being a highly competent and well-run society grew, so did the opportunities. In February 1992, at the invitation of the Building Societies Commission, Northern Rock mounted a rescue for the Lancastrian Building Society which had got into trouble by investing too heavily in estate agents and unwise commercial lending. One of its more unpromising ventures was to put money into the building of a housing estate at the bottom of quarry. On investigation, Northern Rock rapidly reached the conclusion that 'quite simply the Lancastrian Building Society has spent too much money in too short a time trying to be an effective building society.' If it continued, it was likely that the Lancastrian would lose £7 million in the current year with reserves down to just £600,000. It was effectively bankrupt. On the other hand, shutting it down immediately and incorporating it into Northern Rock would bring substantial benefits. And so it proved. The reserves were

Chris Sharp, chief executive from 1982 to 1997.

liquidated to pay off current losses: closing branches, eliminating the head office and getting rid of senior staff reduced costs; while the mortgage book added to Northern Rock's strength in the north-west. It was, in effect, a government-licensed, asset-stripping operation.

It was not long before other targets came into view. In July 1992 the board debated the pros and cons of a merger with the Britannia Building Society which had started life as the Leek and Moorlands Permanent Benefit Society in 1856, and later became the Leek and Westbourne, and finally reinvented itself as the Britannia in 1975. Under the influence of Sir Hubert Newton, one of the grand old men of the building society movement, it had become the ninth largest building society in the UK with assets of £9,000 million. But Northern Rock was catching up fast. In the course of 1992, its assets would grow by an astonishing 36.3 per cent to just over £6,000 million, which meant the society was expanding twice as fast as any other. It was a performance that put Northern Rock just outside the top ten. It is little wonder that the society won *Which* magazine's award that year for the best regional building society.

The board's discussion about the possible merger with Britannia is interesting for the light it throws on how Northern Rock regarded itself in the early 1990s. There was general agreement that the society's distribution network was too small but much less about what should be done about it. The chairman, Lord Ridley, led the revolt against the Britannia, supported by Sir John Riddell, who had recently returned after a stint as private secretary to Prince Charles and Princess Diana. Sir John said that he had no desire to be part of 'a frightfully boring society in a frightfully boring place (like Leek)'. Did the directors want, he asked mischievously, 'to remain part of what might be seen as an extremely small (sic) Newcastle operation, or would they prefer to be leading figures in revitalising – à la Mary Rose – the "old rotting hulks" of the Britannia?' Sir John was adamant that he would never accept Leek as the headquarters of the merged societies but he would settle for Newcastle or, at a pinch, London. His fellow directors concurred. And the idea of a merger with the Britannia quietly faded away.

Building Societies Association and Council of Mortgage Lenders lunch with John Major (centre), Chris Sharp on his left.

The Duke of Kent (left) opened the extension to the Northern Rock House (*facing page*) in April 1991. John Riddell, now chairman, is on the far right, second from the right is Chris Jobe, group secretary.

10

The Road to Conversion

Robert Dickinson, chairman
from 1992 to 1999.

The Britannia deal may have been a non-starter, but the urge to merge remained. In the summer of 1993, Chris Sharp opened negotiations with Mike Jackson, the chief executive of Birmingham Midshires, a society of similar size to Northern Rock. Outwardly, the talks were friendly enough. Sharp conceded that as the younger man, Jackson would eventually run the combined operation. But he insisted that the headquarters should remain in Newcastle, and that the chairman and one other director should be Northern Rock people. Jackson, for his part, insisted that he take over as chief executive straightaway. For the record, Jackson tried to give the impression that his society was a cut above Northern Rock. It is, he wrote, 'our desire to differentiate ourselves on the basis of quality rather than Northern Rock's stated objective of being a low cost provider', but in reality the talks broke down over personalities and a failure to agree about who should do what. Sharp told his colleagues that he found Jackson less than stimulating. A few years later Birmingham Midshires was absorbed by the Halifax.

Even without the Birmingham deal, the society continued to grow at record speed. The results for the first nine months of 1993 revealed the best figures ever with assets up 16.4 per cent to over £7,000 million, and profits in excess of the previous year with three months of the year still to run. The society was not only getting bigger but also stronger. For the second year running it won the *Which?* award for the best regional building society.

Reviewing the 1993 results, Chris Sharp wrote: 'The combination of a rising reserve ratio and a continuing fall in our unit costs is very encouraging. From being one of the most expensive societies to run, we are now at the forefront of the most efficient.' The society's success was beginning to attract attention, some of it unwelcome. In November 1993, Sharp

The Special General Meeting at Newcastle Arena, 15 April 1997,
approved conversion from a mutual society to a public limited company.

The Northern Rock rugby squad, regular championship winners.

Ruby Smith and Graham Hodgson, from Northern Rock, on Community Challenge, helping members of the Leonard Cheshire Trust.

reported an approach from the Bank of Scotland. Unanimously, the board voted to reject it.

Encouraging as the results were, Northern Rock's position was not strong. In essence, the problem was: how could a society as aggressive as Northern Rock continue to develop its mortgage business when the main focus of its activities was in the north and most of the action was in the south? Much had been done to redress the imbalance but even now some 50 per cent of its mortgage business was north of the Trent, with the south accounting for little more than a quarter. A paper on the society's lending plans put its finger on it when it said: 'In geographical terms, the growth will be driven largely from our Midlands and Southern regions, where the major conurbations and new territories give the greatest scope for growth. In contrast the role for the north-east will be twofold: (1) to maintain and defend the very high market share we currently hold and (2) to increase the proportion of direct business we can generate from our existing customers in our home territory.' The society's posture was a judicious mixture of aggression and defence.

Scarcely a month after the presentation of this paper to the board, Leo Finn happened to meet Ron Shiel, chairman of the North of England Building Society at a Christmas party. As well as being business rivals, the two men were good friends. And so when Shiel made an uncharacteristically critical remark about his chief executive, Finn instantly knew something was amiss and suggested a meeting. Early in the new year, Shiel and Finn met at the Gosforth Park Hotel where it became clear that Shiel was so unhappy at what was going on at the Sunderland-based building society that he was in fact inviting Northern Rock to take it over. He told Finn that he had lost confidence in his own management. He suspected that he was not being told what was happening and wanted a dignified way out. The two men agreed that the takeover should be dressed up to look like a union of the two to form a 'Great North Society.' As the chief executive was excluded from the plot, it fell to Leo Finn not only to draft

The naming of a railway engine, with Chris Sharp on the left. In the centre is Nora Preen, in her mid-nineties, the oldest Northern Rock first-time buyer.

his chairman's letter but also Ron Shiel's reply. The project was nicknamed 'Alpha Beta' and there were a number of secret meetings at Styford Hall, the family home of Robert Dickinson, who had taken over as chairman from Lord Ridley in 1992. The son of Roy, Robert Dickinson was the fourth member of the family to serve the society over a period stretching back to the foundation of the Rock in 1865.

On 23 February 1994, Dickinson wrote to Shiel to put forward the idea of a Great North society. 'We believe that the period up to the end of the millennium will bring yet more competition and more balance sheet strain,' he wrote. 'We do not think that well managed and well capitalised Societies will go out of business but there is a distinct possibility that asset growth will be harder to achieve, all income streams including mortgage interest will come under great threat and Societies which do not succeed in the wider financial services or bancassurance market will find it increasingly difficult to compete successfully.' But it was not until he reached his final paragraph that the chairman mentioned the real motive for the approach. 'We are . . . concerned', he concluded, 'that the North of England might at some future date decide to merge with a Society or institution based outside the North East. In the final analysis we are convinced that both Societies together could be the first step towards the creation of a very large building society based in the North East.'

A full month was to elapse before the Northern Rock board was told what was up. After describing his meetings with Shiel, Finn told his fellow directors that the directors of North of England had agreed to receive an outline offer and that it was probable that they would vote in favour in four days time. On paper the deal looked good. With 300,000 investment accounts, 43,000 borrowers, forty-three branches, 400 staff, assets of £1,500 million, including £80 million of reserves, NEBS was no basket case. But with low growth and high management expenses, it was ripe for takeover. Finn calculated that not only would its acquisition propel Northern Rock securely into the Top Ten, but the arithmetic looked very attractive. Even if half the North of England's reserves were set aside to cover potential losses, that still left another £40 million to bolster Northern Rock's own resources, plus an income stream from mortgage payments of £25 to £30 million a

Ron Shiel, chairman of North of England Building Society (left), and Robert Dickinson, chairman of Northern Rock, at the time of the merger.

year. Improving the target society's efficiency and reserve ratios would, so Finn calculated, produce enough cash to pay for all costs. As Finn told the board: 'The price is not high as in strict commercial terms it might well cost £150 million to acquire NEBS and we would be getting it for free whilst preventing entry into our cherished home market.'

Unlike the Britannia and Birmingham Midshires, the NEBS made few demands. It was agreed that there should be jobs for the NEBS deputy managing director and the finance director and that three directors should be offered places on the Northern Rock board as non-executives. In the event, the executive directors left before the marriage was consummated.

The acquisition of the North of England gave Northern Rock the size and financial muscle it was seeking. It confirmed its position as the north's leading building society and propelled it to the top of nearly all the UBS intersociety performance tables, ahead of far bigger competitors like the Halifax, the Leeds, and the Alliance and Leicester. For every indicator but two, Northern Rock was in the top four. As for profitability it was, quite simply, the best. 1994 was the *annus mirabilis*. As Chris Sharp remarked: '1994 was one of the most important years in Northern Rock's long history. Not only has our performance set new records in terms of lending, profit and cost-efficiency, but we have also absorbed one of our local rivals, the North of England, and simultaneously become a Top Ten player, with assets exceeding £10 billion.' Over the past four years, Northern Rock had increased its size threefold, its profits fourfold and had halved its management expense ratios.

This was, however, no time for sitting back and admiring the

Angus Griffin   Christopher Sharp   Ronald Shiel   Robert Dickinson   Robert Linden   Leo

North of England Building
Society merger announcement,
3 April 1996.

paintwork. Northern Rock had barely completed shoring up its defences when there were some alarming developments. The takeovers of the Cheltenham and Gloucester by Lloyds Bank and the acquisition of the Leeds Building Society by the Halifax had opened building society members' eyes to the wealth that was locked away inside the mutuals – wealth that, in theory, belonged to them. But worse was to come. In April 1995 the news broke that the Abbey National was making a takeover bid for the National and Provincial. The Abbey had timed its bid at the precise psychological moment when it thought that the National and Provincial members would be at their most receptive. The approach was made immediately after the collapse of the National and Provincial's merger talks with the Leeds and days before N&P's annual general meeting. An indication of how things might go came from one N&P member, a retired lecturer called Keith Porter, who was quoted as saying: 'Everybody has a price. Mine would be about £500.'

Direct appeals to shareholders are the common currency of City takeovers but it was something new in the cosy world of building societies. The Abbey's move caused the Northern Rock board rapidly to reappraise the situation. In a paper to the board, Leo Finn rapidly concluded that 'the probability of a hostile bid from another building society for a classic merger is zero. No society has the spare capital.' Nor, he thought, would a banking predator stand much chance of success. 'The predator who had done his homework would quickly realise that the forced acquisition of a building society would rival Jarndyce v. Jarndyce as a piece of costly theatre and would be unlikely to attempt it.' 'The only viable attack on us', Finn argued, 'would come in the form of a press campaign which offered our members large cash payments in return for votes at a General Meeting.'

Customer consultant Liz Marshall, from North Shields branch, gives up-to-the-minute information to a customer.

After discussing various forms of defence, Finn raised the possibility of converting the society into a plc. However, the idea was mentioned only in passing as a long-term option and Finn moved quickly on to other subjects.

It was not through loyalty to 150 years of mutuality that the management hesitated to push the conversion option. 'I do not think that the defence of mutuality per se is worth running,' Finn told the board. 'It's merely a Victorian form of incorporation and we cannot demonstrate that we behave "mutually" . . . We run our business to optimise profit levels . . . We must do so to protect investors' funds, please credit rating agencies and satisfy supervisors – just as banks do.' The reason why the society was nervous about conversion was that it feared it would open the door to a predator. 'We thought that if we were to do this, it would put us immediately in play,' says Robert Dickinson. 'It was alright for the Abbey National or the Halifax but as a smaller society we would have been gobbled up just like the National and Provincial.'

In the summer of 1995, Finn did the rounds of the City asking merchant banks for advice. 'All the banks we went to see told us that building societies were finished and they all tried to persuade us to give up. But when it came to talking about how we might defend ourselves, nobody came up with a single good idea. So we said: "If one of your clients bids for us, we will ensure we do not recommend them to our members."' What changed the picture was a visit Finn made in August to Terry Eccles and David White of J. P. Morgan. There he learnt how the bank had helped a Scandinavian trustee savings bank which, like Northern Rock, wanted to float but was looking for protection against takeover. Morgan's solution was to sell a substantial portion of the shares to the local community. Why not, the bankers suggested, do something similar with Northern Rock? Morgan argued that Northern Rock would get the best of both worlds. 'It allows you to maintain all that you believe in as regards history and so forth. But you also become part of a much more interesting world,' the bankers said. And they proposed that up to 30 per cent of the shares should be set aside in some form or other.

Finn was very excited by this idea. Shortly after the meeting at Morgans, he went on a family holiday to Umbria with Chris Sharp, taking the Morgan presentation with him. As Finn remembers, the first ten days were spent eating, drinking and relaxing around the pool. But on about day eleven, he managed to persuade Sharp to look at the bank's proposal. Sharp too was enthusiastic. And on their return, they told Robert Dickinson about the developments and took soundings from the executive directors. Not everybody was as enthusiastic as the top three. Lord Howick, a non-executive director, in particular, strongly questioned the wisdom of abandoning mutuality. 'There were no secret meetings in corridors,' says Finn. 'Everything was out in the open. We had to persuade the board and most of them were persuaded. We won the arguments on its merits.' But Finn admits that the balance of power in the boardroom was tipped in favour of management. 'By that time management was quite powerful,' he says. 'We were acknowledged to be the most successful building society in the UK. Chris was a hugely powerful chief executive. We had just engineered the North of England deal. So we were a hell of a group to take on.'

Chris Sharp checking the conversion document as it comes off the press, April 1997.

It was the idea of a Northern Rock Charitable Foundation that swung the board round. In discussions, the idea emerged that instead of selling part of the company to the local community, as the Swedes had, 15 per cent of the issued share capital and 5 per cent of the new plc's annual profit should be used to set up a charitable foundation to support good causes, principally in the north-east. On 19 December 1995, the proposal to convert to a plc was formally put to the board by Robert Dickinson. Management had prepared the ground well. After a short discussion on logistics, the board gave the go-ahead for a proposal which, it thought, would be 'a credible vehicle for maintaining a caring, independent, north-east-based financial institution for at least five years whilst at the same time recognising and unbundling the interests of members.' Discussions continued well into the spring of 1996 but essentially the die had been cast. On 3 April the news was broken that the society would cease to be a building society on 1 October 1997.

The next 18 months was a period of intense activity for everybody. There was a brief clash between Chris Sharp and Adrian Coles, the director general of the BSA, after Coles had publicly criticised the converting building societies on the BBC's Moneycheck programme. 'The BSA doesn't represent those societies,' he said. In response Sharp wrote a memo to the board recommending Northern Rock's resignation from the BSA in which he said 'he could see no reason why we should contribute to the salary of a director general who was not speaking for us but who was actually speaking against us'.

That incident apart, the conversion exercise, though arduous, went remarkably smoothly. The climax came at a special general meeting on 15 April 1997. Just to be on the safe side Northern Rock had booked the Newcastle Arena. Seating 11,000, it is a popular

Directors on the Tyne Bridge on the day of the flotation. From left to right: Adam Applegarth (executive director), Bob Bennett (finance director), Robert Dickinson (chairman), Leo Finn (chief executive), and David Baker (executive director).

venue for rock concerts and other shows. But on this occasion, there was ample spare capacity. The final chapter was a special meeting of the Northern Rock Building Society which had at the time some 900,000 members. It was attended by a total 470 people, the full sixteen-man board, 394 investors and sixty borrowing members. The meeting was told that of the 700,000 investors and borrowers who had voted, 680,000 were in favour. In all some 450 million shares were issued. Each person, on average, received 500 shares, worth £2,250 at an issue price of 452p. Demand for shares was oversubscribed 3.3 times and the cost of the conversion exercise came to £32.4 million – almost exactly in line with the original estimate.

The one sadness in the midst of the celebrations was that Chris Sharp was not there for what would have been the high point of his highly successful working life. On 8 May 1997, just three weeks after the special general meeting, he died of a heart attack. His friend and close colleague, Leo Finn, was appointed the same morning to succeed him. In a tribute on behalf of his colleagues and friends, David Baker said:

Fiona Ellis, director of the Northern Rock Foundation, at the launch in January 1998.

> Chris Sharp was regarded with such huge affection by everyone who worked for him and with him. He was an extremely popular man of huge intellect and integrity, and he inspired people as a great leader of Northern Rock over the past 15 years. Although he was not a Geordie by birth he became one by adoption and he had a great love for the north-east. He worked tirelessly on its behalf, promoting it as a place to live and work. He enjoyed being involved in so many aspects of the life of the region. Most of all his pride was to have established Northern Rock as the major financial company based in the north-east. His great desire to complete the conversion to a plc was to ensure it would remain as an independent force based in Newcastle. That is his legacy and that is now what we will put in place.

Leo Finn, chief executive since 1997.

Perhaps the most enduring legacy of all is the Northern Rock Foundation. Established by Northern Rock plc, each year the foundation receives some 5 per cent of the company's consolidated pre-tax profits. By the end of 1999, the Foundation had received a total of £22.7 million, of which over £11 million had been given away to over 500 good causes throughout the north-east and beyond.

The individual grants ranged from £250,000 towards building a nursery for very young children of deprived families in the Scotswood district of Newcastle, to £1,000 to protect the homes of elderly people in the Sunderland, Washington and Houghton-le-Spring areas against burglary. As the Foundation grows in confidence and experience, so its programmes have become more ambitious. Its Coalfields project is intended to support local people living in the villages and towns of the coalfield communities of County Durham,

Northumberland, Gateshead, Sunderland and South Tyneside. By the end of 1999, the trustees had awarded £1.2 million to 41 coalfield projects that were thought to offer a lasting benefit to a town or village. At Newbiggin-by-the-Sea, £50,000 is being spent to create 20 modern apprenticeships in engineering by means of a boat-building programme with Northumberland College, while in Shilbottle, £25,000 has gone on new equipment for a skills centre.

Strictly speaking, the Foundation is the offspring of Northern Rock plc. But as an organisation devoted to the well-being of the people of Durham,

Northumberland, Teeside and Tyne and Wear, its origins lie much further back, in the days, a century and a half ago, which saw the birth of the Northern Counties Building Society. In its manifesto, the Northern Counties set out to help the poorer and more disadvantaged people to find a home and build a better life for themselves and their families. So too does the Northern Rock Foundation. Our story, which started with the creation of the Northern Counties and the Rock, ends at the point when the Northern Rock ceased to be a building society. But the tradition of care and concern for the region and its people lives on. The wheel has come full circle.

Robert Dickinson and his
successor as chairman,
Sir John Riddell, 1999.

Continuing to Build

The transformation of Northern Rock into a public company was a huge success. Over 43 per cent of the shares in issue were sold to institutions in a single auction that was three times oversubscribed. All qualifying members received a windfall of 500 shares worth £2,250 and the shops and travels agencies of Tyneside and Wearside had a welcome mini boom.

Since October 1997 Northern Rock has settled into the routine of being a public company. Interim and final results are accompanied by meetings with analysts and shareholders and inevitably the company has had a much higher public profile.

In the three years since the flotation there has been dramatic change in the market. There has been more demutalisation, and carpet-bagging – investing for the sake of a windfall – became a national pastime. Building societies have been forced to work lower margins as they have defended their status by paying members mutuality bonuses. Northern Rock has continued to grow its assets and its profits. It is still the most efficient player in the mortgage market and is readily adapting to the huge changes brought on by the advent of the Internet and digital television.

The company remains confident that it will be a leading participant in the UK lending market by fulfilling its strategic vision of a virtuous circle – the growth of assets exceeding the growth of costs which provides a reduction of unit cost to be divided between better products for customers and greater returns for shareholders.

Leo Finn, Chief Executive

The Northern Rock board and
senior management, 2000.

Index

Numbers in **bold** refer to illustrations